FROM THE TOP

ALSO BY MICHAEL PERRY

BOOKS

Visiting Tom: A Man, a Highway, and the Road to Roughneck Grace

Coop: A Year of Poultry, Pigs, and Parenting

Truck: A Love Story

Population: 485: Meeting Your Neighbors One Siren at a Time

Off Main Street: Barnstormers, Prophets and Gatemouth's Gator

Big Rigs, Elvis & The Grand Dragon Wayne

Why They Killed Big Boy

AUDIO

The Clodhopper Monologues

Never Stand Behind a Sneezing Cow

I Got It from the Cows

MUSIC

Headwinded (Michael Perry and the Long Beds)

Tiny Pilot (Michael Perry and the Long Beds)

MICHAEL PERRY

From

THE TOP

BRIEF TRANSMISSIONS FROM
TENT SHOW RADIO

Ballyhoo!

WISCONSIN HISTORICAL SOCIETY PRESS

Published by the Wisconsin Historical Society Press
Publishers since 1855

Text copyright © Michael Perry 2013

Portions of this book are adapted from material previously published by
HarperCollins and in *Men's Health* and the *Wisconsin State Journal.*

For permission to reuse material from *From the Top* (ISBN 978-0-87020-680-1;
e-book ISBN 978-0-87020-681-8), please access www.copyright.com or contact
the Copyright Clearance Center, Inc. (CCC), 222 Rosewood Drive, Danvers,
MA 01923, 978-750-8400. CCC is a not-for-profit organization that provides
licenses and registration for a variety of users.

wisconsin history.org

Printed in Wisconsin, USA
Designed by Percolator Graphic Design
17 16 15 14 13   1 2 3 4 5

Library of Congress Cataloging-in-Publication Data
Perry, Michael, 1964–
   From the top : brief transmissions from Tent Show Radio / Michael Perry.
      pages cm
   ISBN 978-0-87020-680-1 (pbk.) — ISBN 978-0-87020-681-8 (e-book)
1. Perry, Michael, 1964—Anecdotes. 2. Tent show radio (Radio program)
I. Title.
   AC8.P577 2013
   814'.6—dc23

                                                                    2013041080

♾ The paper used in this publication meets the minimum requirements of the
American National Standard for Information Sciences—Permanence of Paper
for Printed Library Materials, ANSI Z39.48-1992.

To the founders of Lake Superior Big Top Chautauqua.
They raised this tent in every sense.

To the volunteers.
If you're at a show and see someone
in a blue vest, please thank them.

And to the audience.
It's empty without you.

CONTENTS

THE INNER CIRCLE

A SENSE OF PITCH

LOCK UP THE CHICKENS

FRIENDS AND NEIGHBORS

INTRODUCTION

······································

Ah, it's great to be way up north here under the beautiful blue and pearl-gray canvas, this fine, stout tent at the foot of Mount Ashwabay, overlooking the ancient waters surrounding the Apostle Islands and just one sailful of breeze away from Chequamegon Bay.

The performance you're about to hear is one in a long, long tradition of singing, dancing, and storytelling performed live and in person beneath this beautiful tent. We keep 'er pitched from June until the autumn moons, and we'd be most grateful if you choose to join us; you'll find a complete schedule at bigtop.org. We hope you join us, and if you do, when the first note rises from the stage we think you'll understand why patrons and performers alike love to say: Big Top Chautauqua . . . it's the Carnegie Hall of Tent Shows.

For the past three years it has been my privilege to approach a microphone and recite those words as the host of *Tent Show Radio*, a production originating from a spacious canvas tent pitched at the base of a ski hill overlooking Lake Superior in northern Wisconsin.

I invoke the term *privilege* with specific intent. The history of Lake Superior Big Top Chautauqua extends back over a quarter-century now, and I am a late arrival. The tent didn't pitch itself. It was raised by a small band of freethinking optimists, and every time I step to the microphone I keep that in mind. I offer the contents of this book not from a position of propriety but rather as a grateful guest. I'm just a guy allowed to sneak in through the backstage flap now and then.

• • •

The best seat in the Lake Superior Big Top Chautauqua tent is not for sale. I don't say that to be snooty or snotty, I'm just letting you know the way it is. Don't obsess over it, because the seat is located in a section theater professionals refer to as "obstructed view"—so obstructed, in fact, that you can't even see the show from there. The spot in question is situated in a brace of old drop-down theater chairs set up along the backstage walkway between the stage and the dressing rooms.

It's cozy back there, and quiet. From this seat you can see the artists preparing to take the stage. Some are "one-namers"—so famous they're recognized worldwide by their first name alone. Some should be famous but are not, and some are making their first stage appearance ever. Actors shuffle to and fro, muttering their lines. Black-clad stagehands hurry through, bound to set a last-minute prop or string a mic cord. You'll see a musician leaning in to bring his guitar in tune, or a vocalist, her throat wrapped in scarves, hunched in a chair and cupping a mug of honey-lemon tea. Novice performers pace back and forth, checking and rechecking the dry-erase board for curtain times. Veteran performers check email or discuss health insurance deductibles. The lights are low, and everyone is getting ready for the show.

I especially cherish this seat on those nippy nights early in the spring season or in the final few weeks before strike, because the crew keeps a pot of good coffee going just off the wings stage right, and the smell is even better because of the edge in the air. It's enchanting to sit in that theater chair and observe this charmed space where performers take one last deep breath before heading out to the lights and applause. Sometimes they leave behind hints of their preparation: a scribbled set list, a curled and highlighted page of script, a cellphone still glowing with the last number dialed being the number home.

Then the show begins, and even from back here you can feel the electric momentum of it, the way the performer and audience agree to dive in and see what happens. Sitting in the suddenly empty backstage space you can hear little things that don't go

out over the sound system—the scuff and twist of a dancer's
slipper, the thump of a musician's heel keeping time, the creak of
the stage as an actor crosses. You can see into the tangle of cords
and girders beneath the stage where an electronic light blinks,
relaying some information that means something to someone,
and then—and this is the best, best part of all—through a gap in
the velvet skirt at the stage front come distinct sounds from the
audience: an anticipatory titter, an appreciative gasp, an over-
loud clapper, and sometimes, when the performer has drawn
a tent full of strangers deep into the center of the moment, the
fragile, expectant silence.

• • •

Many of these shows—even the silent bits—are recorded and put
together for broadcast on *Tent Show Radio.* My job is to introduce
the show, close the show, and during intermission—right in the
middle there—have a little talk about anything I wish. Those little
talks are what led to the book in your hands.

As a writer I'm used to working in long form over a long time:
essays that take weeks to finish, magazine pieces that take months,
books that take years. Thousands, tens of thousands, hundreds
of thousands of words. *Tent Show Radio* monologues, however,
have to be written once a week and must be brief enough to fit the
six-minute sandwich between two thick slices of music. I've been
typing for a while now, and it's been a challenge to find my voice in
this format. I have also renewed my respect (established twenty
years ago when I worked as a newspaper stringer) for anyone—
be they plumber or poet—who produces under tight deadlines.
(In fact, the radio show monologues led directly to a gig writing
a weekly column for the *Wisconsin State Journal,* an opportunity
for which I am grateful and baggy-eyed.) When preparing these
brief transmissions, I strive for a more conversational tone and
spend less time excavating the ol' thesaurus.

I was invited to host *Tent Show Radio* in part because of my
books, which I drew on for many of the early show monologues.

I also often try out material on stage or in the recording studio before I commit it to print. All this is to say, you may recognize some of these stories in whole or in part.

For the purposes of this book I have tuned a few things. For one, I've restored a lot of gerunds. Folksiness tends to play better on the ear than the eye, and even then I've been known to overdo it. For the most part I've also stripped out certain prefatory and referential comments that become repetitive or make little sense outside the show. That said, I've left in quite a few *anyways*es, as in, "So, anyways . . . ," as that is just the way we talk around here.

Not every *Tent Show Radio* monologue made the cut, and rather than run them in order of their original broadcast, I grouped them in loosely thematic clusters. You can read the book backward if you wish. Or scattershot. I've navigated much of my life in exactly that manner.

I hope you enjoy the pieces. And I hope you enjoy the radio show. But most of all I hope one day you have a chance to enjoy a show inside the Big Top itself. If you have the desire and constitution, I recommend you arrive early and hike to the top of Mount Ashwabay. Don't look back until you're all the way up there where the skiers unload from the lift. Then turn, and you will see the picture I try to paint every single time I introduce *Tent Show Radio*: the tent, plopped high atop the land like an Alice in Wonderland pearl-gray-and-blue-striped mushroom, a benevolent psychedelic aberration amidst swathes of verdant green sloping to a backdrop of Great Lakes blue, the distant water dappled by a scatter of treasured islands.

What a place to see a show.

A FINE PLACE TO START

One of the great freedoms of the *Tent Show Radio* format is that I am allowed to ramble on about whatever comes to mind: oddly shod loggers, my last cup of coffee, love and lost fingers, useful cheaters, gratitude, and guys who get gozzled.

Also, timeless infinity.

And Victoria's Secret.

In the same essay.

VICTORIA'S SECRET AND THE COSMOS

Lately I have been contemplating the cosmos, which is to say standing out behind the chicken coop after battening the hatches for the evening and staring at the stars. You can see the stars pretty good out back of the coop if you look down the ridge, where there's nothing but one mercury vapor farm yard light in the distance. If you look off to the north you won't see quite as many stars because someone built a big house off that way and put up their own faux vintage streetlights to line the driveway and then additionally surrounded the house with a row of halogens apparently uprooted from the runway at Chicago's O'Hare airport. No sense building a place like that if folks can't admire it all night long, I guess. And then off to the northwest, well, it's tough to see any stars at all because the horizon is always gauzy white from the glow of the parking lot lights over at the mall. It can be odd sometimes, standing in the pig pen knowing you're less than ten minutes from the fall collection at Victoria's Secret.

The lights keep coming closer, and I suppose unless the Mayans were bad at math they'll keep coming. There's no sense in me getting too snippy about it, since I'm part of that parade. Our house began as a log cabin built in the 1880s, and you know for a fact the first time an Ojibwe or a trapper looked up the hill and saw a lantern in the window they figured there goes the dang neighborhood, and in truth whenever we say that we're generally right. In a small gesture of nocturnal regard, when our mercury vapor yard light burned out I left it that way, but that was less about me taking a stand against light pollution than me taking a stand against climbing ladders anywhere near power lines.

The other reason I don't get too snippy is because when we get snippy we tend to snip ourselves right in our own behinds. I still get letters and emails from readers who tell me how much they enjoyed the essay I wrote back in 1996 taking to task people who live in houses built atop hills, and as I read those emails and letters now in our *house atop a hill,* I pause to consider the view and reflect on my own inconsistencies. I didn't build this house up here, and you can hardly call an old mismatched, slant-floored, crooked-windowed farmhouse ostentatious, but nonetheless the paradox is sufficient to tap my self-regard on the shoulder and give me that look that says, *Umm, take 'er down a notch.*

So I stand out there behind the coop, and I look at the stars, and I pick out the constellations, going through them one by one: Orion . . . the Big Dipper . . . the North Star . . . aaand that's it, 'cause I don't know any more unless I fire up the iPad app. But even staring up and out at the stars in ignorance is worth my while because we can all use some cosmic recalibration now and then. And nothing calibrates your snippy, nothing tempers your self-regard, nothing tamps down your own ego like thirty seconds spent staring into a depthless universe of countless howling gas balls. In a darker form of comfort, when I lower my gaze and reencounter the encroaching lights of creeping humankind, I am re-reminded that we could pave and streetlight this entire blue ball and still not be so much as a blink against what's out there and furthermore the universe is capable of shutting us down in an instant, in the manner of someone triggering a Cosmic Clapper. But then my heart becomes cozier as I look back over my shoulder to the glow of the mall and realize that despite all the black holes in the universe, I have managed somehow in this instant to place myself in perfect equidistance between timeless infinity and Victoria's Secret.

TEETOTAL

I have never had a beer. Or a shot. Or a glass of wine. I did chug some high-octane cough syrup when I was a tot (Mom kept a bottle of stuff that tasted like crushed pine needles). And once in my youth after digging the last spoonful of chocolate syrup out of an ice cream cup at a wedding reception, I was surprised to find it tasted bitter. I sat there with my head tilted quizzically for a second only to realize as it slid down my gullet that I had just ingested demon rum. So perhaps I can't claim to be a total teetotal, but those few teaspoons represent the lifelong sum of my recreational boozing.

Whenever someone offers me a drink and I decline, they invariably react in one of two ways. Some back away with eyes wide and hands spread in a "no harm, no foul" stance, saying, "Okay, that's cool, no worries," clearly thinking they're about to receive a temperance lecture. More commonly, the person pauses, then—as the false realization dawns—says "Ohhh" and surreptitiously slides his own drink out of sight while giving me a meaningful nod to acknowledge my struggle for sobriety.

Truth is, I just don't drink.

Once after a romantic shipwreck that had me all mopey, I accompanied my friend Al—a connoisseur of small-town bars, cigars, and cold beer—to a local tavern. As I spilled out my troubles and toyed with my water glass, Al listened patiently. I confessed that I was finally tempted to begin drinking.

"Oh, Mikey . . ." said Al, in the tenderest of tones. "There would never be a better time to start!" Raising his beer and displaying it on the open palm of his other hand in the manner of a game show hostess presenting a prize, he said, "Happiness in a can, my friend, happiness in a can."

After reading several reports by experts touting the health benefits of moderate alcohol consumption, I finally turned to the one person who is an expert on me: my wife. Anneliese is a moderate drinker and nutrition fanatic. "Do you think I should start drinking?" I asked, to which she replied, "Not if you handle your drinking anything like you handle your sugar." Recently she has been forced to hide her baking supplies (specifically, the chocolate chip bag) in the freezer beneath a fortress of pork chops. I know because that's where I found them last Tuesday at 3 a.m. Those were harsh words from the one I love, but having weighed the available research against the limits of my willpower and all other options, I'm going to stay on the wagon. After all these years it'd be a shame to find out I'm the guy who can't hold his booze. Nothing sadder than a fellow my age woo-hooing in a sports bar.

Besides, the abstemious life has its upside. First time I was ever called to jury duty, it was for a guy fighting a drunk-driving case. Having responded as an EMT to alcohol-related crashes for years, and having worked at least one accident scene with the arresting deputy, I figured I'd be rejected right away. But I made it into the final group and was seated. Just as the judge swiveled to begin the trial, he paused and swiveled back to look at us in the jury box. "Just out of curiosity," he said, "is there anyone of you who doesn't drink?"

I raised my hand. I was the only one.

"Do you believe if someone drinks alcohol they are a bad person?" asked the judge.

"If I did," I replied, "I wouldn't have any friends."

That got a pretty good laugh, but then the judge one-upped me.

"Not in this county you wouldn't."

That got an even bigger laugh.

And then he bounced me off the jury.

I considered stopping at a tavern on the way home, but crying in your near-beer just doesn't cut it.

HERE WE GO AGAIN

Not long ago I was regaling my wife with a gripping anecdote when her eyes glazed over even more quickly than usual. I tapered off and then said, "Umm . . . did I tell you that one before?" And she said, "Yes, honey," which if you've been married for any length of time at all you know is longsuffering wifespeak for "seven times, minimum."

Recently I had an apparently deep thought. At least I thought it was deep. In other words, I was in up to my ankles. Anyways, I scribbled it down quick before it could escape through the air holes in my head. Then I took to polishing it like the precious gem it was. I caressed it and I furbished it and I thesaurused it and I turned it this way and that way and I built it up and I shaved it down and rounded off the edges and then I threw a little sparkle on it, and when I was done I congratulated myself on what was clearly a rare nugget of original profundity. About a week later I was pawing through some old papers and found I had written the exact same thing, pretty much word for word, in an essay seven years earlier.

Point is, whether I'm writing, telling a story, or just shooting the breeze, I'm afraid I've hit that stage in my life where every time I open my mouth I'm either repeating myself or contradicting myself.

We all develop these little tics over time. For instance, I'm forever using the word *little*. I wish you wouldn't pay attention, but if you do, you'll see that the word *little* pops up like Whac-A-Mole in my conversations and in my first drafts. These days as soon as I finish a rough draft I perform a search-and-replace maneuver whereby I replace every *little* with nothing.

I have the same problem with another phrase. As a matter of fact, I use this phrase so often that even though I'm a teetotal, I've come up with what I call the Michael Perry So Anyways Drinking game. How it works is, anytime you're talking to me—or more specifically, I'm talking to, through, or past you—every time I go, "So, anyways . . . ," why, you take a slug. I don't care if your liver is made of steel wool and Teflon, you'll be flat on your back before I get to the point.

Some of you know I've been privileged to serve as an emergency medical technician and first responder for the previous few decades. Once when I was on call with my brother, we picked up an elderly lady from the Alzheimer's wing of the nursing home. She had become agitated and attacked another patient and was being transferred to a psychiatric hospital for evaluation. She was very nervous and worked up, asking me the same questions over and over. "Where are you taking me?" "Don't you hurt me!" "I want to see my doctor!" "Who is my doctor?" I answered her gently, over and over, the same answers every time. "We're going to the hospital." "No, Betty, no one will hurt you." "We'll see your doctor as soon as we get to the hospital." "Your doctor is Dr. Jackson."

She repeated the cycle of identical questions about fifteen times. Each time, I answered exactly the same, always maintaining eye contact. It seemed to reassure her. She became calmer. About ten minutes into the ride, she started the cycle again. "Where are you taking me?"

"We're going to the hospital."

Something changed in her eyes. A little slyness, a little exasperation.

"Well, I know," she said. "You said that fifteen times now!"

My wife knows exactly how she feels.

The thing is, storytellers—and I include singers and writers in the group, as well as that lady at the café and Burt down there to the feed mill—storytellers like to think of themselves as bards and troubadours and raconteurs entrusted with the preservation of our precious oral traditions. Y'know, I like the idea of that myself. But then I'll be a few minutes into a story and I'll see my wife's eyes go, and I'll realize I'm not engaged in the preservation of precious oral traditions, I'm engaged in recycling.

RE-DECAFFEINATED

I've been quitting coffee again.

I don't really remember where I got started on coffee. I grew up with Scandihoovians who always shook their heads and marveled at the strength of their brew, which they made in stovetop—and later plug-in—percolators. These were dear, honest, and hardworking folk, but truth is, time has shown me that the stuff they were drinking was mud puddle cream compared to your standard Venti-Schmenti Grandioso currently available at even your most average strip mall beanery.

I have no idea how I got started on coffee, only that by the time I was in nursing school (that's right, citizens, I remain a fully licensed registered nurse in the state of Wisconsin, a matter of concern for the populace in general and the Board of Health in particular) I would slink into the back row of the clinical pharmacology lecture hall with a full thermos and have it gone by lunch break, then have another carafe or two later at home. Surely I must have been constantly thrumming.

I was living with my grandparents at the time and was using what Grandma had in the cupboard, which was your garbage-pail-sized Folgers tin with the plastic lid and the yellow teardrop scooper. This being prior to the age of the personal European cappuccino blaster, I brewed up in Grandma's Mister Coffee purchased on sale at Sears.

Sometime in the early '90s I wound up hanging around poets, and as a direct side effect wound up pensively moping in a coffee shop. There it was I had my first cafe mocha and my first double Americano and my first cappuccino (and learned that "expresso" is actually "espresso"), but more than that, I had my first real good coffee.

And man, I have been ruined ever since. I don't drink, I don't smoke, I'm not snobbish about high-tone culture nor couture, but sitting here in my logger boots I do have to admit that when it comes to coffee I am doubly guilty: on the first hand that I have a caffeine addiction; on the second that I am addicted to the good stuff. If it wasn't a whole bean two minutes ago I don't want it in my cup now—that kind of snobbery. Should that coffee touch plastic or cheap steel en route to my lips, my nose curls up like a debutante who found a stinkbug in her wrist corsage. And the cup? If it's not ceramic—or, oddly enough, paper, which seems to somehow preserve and enhance the bouquet—it's all I can do to choke it down my gullet like some poncey prince forced to snort the commoner's grog. That said, the addiction does win out in the end—if I'm truly jonesing, I'll down any old slop.

Shamed by coffee breath and trembling, now and then I go on these purification binges. Two years ago I went cold turkey, took three consecutive aspirins to ward off the eyeball headache, and then stayed clean and calm for ninety days. But the craving never stopped. When I ground that first batch of relapse beans I wasn't even apologetic, and when I popped the lid on the grinder and sniffed, I coulda just flopped over and kicked my hind leg like a dog.

I've been on the juice mostly ever since. But now and then I notice I'm upping the beans to where they're in danger of overflowing the grinder, and even worse, I notice that the hit just isn't what it was, and then I realize it's time to re-titrate, and I grind that last batch and then don't replace it, and oh, come the morning it is desperate times, the chewing of the stray bean found behind the water boiler, the sniffing of the empty Fair Trade bag, the dream of the next cup. Usually I can stick with it a week or three and then I go swooning straight back to the warm, redolent arms of my steamy mistress, and man, it's always so good to see her.

THE BIG THANKFUL

I've lately been feeling mortal, which sounds like a grim thing but is actually a good thing, and above all a true thing. A simple fact thing.

I'm at that stage in life where I can still be—and ought to be—grateful for my health. But I'm also accumulating a fair collection of hitches and hangups and occasional physiological hiccups of the sort that every now and again tap me on the shoulder as if to say, "Breathe deep, pal. And breathe well. And on the exhale, send up a thank you."

It's that thank you that's been on my mind. It seems to me the only sort of lasting credit we can establish. Whether you send it up from a church pew or a drum circle or a deer stand or just whisper it toward the plaster ceiling on a winter night, you're hoping the words find a home out there in the unknown. Let the record show, your heart is saying, that I was blessed and said so.

Sometimes I say my cosmic thank yous right out loud, maybe even more than I should. I don't mean I tip my head back and holler "Thank you!" at the post office ceiling, or utter audible gratitudes to the cosmos from the produce aisle. I'm far too genetically saturated with stoic Scandinavianism to engage in that sort of untoward exhibitionism, which furthermore can get you kicked out of the grocery store. But in the company of friends and loved ones, I often find myself compelled to wedge in some reference to the fact that if for some reason tomorrow found me deleted from the mortal map, I have had a better life than I ever might have hoped, and don't weep for me Argentina—or Chippewa County. I intend these modest outbursts to serve a double purpose. First, I am indeed a fortunate knucklehead in that I've been mostly free to wander as I please through this life, and any life that involves freedom is not to be lived under assumption.

Second, and perhaps this is not the purest motivation and indeed may be more superstitious than soulful, the thank you serves as a preemptive strike against fate: the thank you is in and of itself an acknowledgment of the possible pending runaway train or silently deforming cell cluster. You say thank you for all you have been given so that tomorrow if you are given nothing you can still look death in the eye and say, "I won."

As in all things, you can overdo the cosmic thank yous, and timing is everything. Just last night at supper my brother and I got to talking on this theme, and I said, "Yah, if I get hit by a truck tomorrow, I can't really complain." My brother nodded his head and chuckled in agreement. Meanwhile, our wives looked at us like we'd drunk gravy straight from the boat. Then there was the time I left on short notice to climb a decidedly nonmetaphorical mountain that had already that year claimed the life of seven people. After I hugged and held my two daughters—one still an infant—my wife walked me to the car and halfway down the sidewalk I felt compelled to tell her that if "anything happened" I was thankful for all life had given me, including her and our children. I don't know what I was expecting, but the look on her face made me think that while this might be a perfectly lovely thing to say, it's probably better said while watching a sunset but maybe not so much as you toodle out the driveway to do something dangerous you've never done before, being a flat-footed flatlander and all.

And yet only days later I found myself hung up in deteriorating conditions and forced to go off trail and make a traverse between two depthless crevasses. For a deathly brittle half hour I felt with every step like I was crossing the Gorge of Death on a bridge made of saltines. Midway across the most dangerous stretch one of the crevasses calved off a chunk the size of a city bus, and the faces of my wife and daughters conjured themselves before me, hovering above the snow, and the thing that kept me calm during that whole ordeal was the memory of my clunky sidewalk thank you, which now I knew had been exactly the right thing to do.

AVULSION AVERSION

I recently removed my wedding ring and hung it on a pin stuck in the corkboard beside the telephone. Throw in teardrops and an empty beer can and you'd have the first verse of a country music song about love gone wrong. But this was unrelated to the state of my marriage, which according to my most recent performance review remains on solid footing—although I never forget that when it comes to the maintenance of matrimony the probationary period is perpetual.

No, I removed the ring in memory of Eric Teanecker's finger, last seen one summer day some twenty-five years ago when several of us employed at the local roller rink (Eric was the manager and DJ, I worked parking lot security and did the hokey-pokey in a Snoopy suit) got together for an afternoon of waterskiing. When it came Eric's turn to ski, he placed his left hand on the gunnel of the ski boat and leapt into the water. Relieved of his weight, the boat rocked up as Eric dropped down. By chance, at that same instant Eric's wedding band caught on the stud of a tarp snap, and when he surfaced he announced that we needed to go to the hospital. I took one look at what was left of his ring finger and agreed. The finger did not survive.

Later, as an EMT and a nurse, I would learn that this type of injury happens frequently enough that it has a name: ring avulsion. Truckers suffer them when a ring snags as they jump down from the cab, and mechanics have been known to get them while withdrawing a hand from the engine compartment to reach for a wrench. This is also why athletes either tape or remove their rings. In particular you must always remove your wedding ring before you dunk a basketball lest it become hung on the hoop or entangled in the net. At a flat-footed five-foot-eight with the vertical leap of a stomped Dixie Cup, I have never needed to take that particular precaution.

However, shortly after we moved to our farm I was yanking hog panels from the weeds when I hooked my ring on one of the protruding galvanized steel rods. I managed to get away with just an uncomfortable pinch and bruise, but I thought immediately of Eric Teanecker. I pulled off my ring and dropped it in my pants pocket. Now whenever I have to move hog panels or drive fence posts or climb on and off machinery or perform work where my hands are moving around anything other than a coffee cup and a keyboard, I remove my ring and hang it on that pin by the phone.

I'm realizing now that perhaps you haven't heard a thing I've said since back there when I mentioned the term *ring avulsion,* at which point I left the light-rail line of humorous reflection and plowed locomotivelike into the genre of graphic public service announcement. This really is a departure from the usual intro- spective chuckle. And yet now that we're here, and as I think of how I care for you all, and how many of you out there work with your hands, I believe I'm glad we're having this one-sided talk. Y'know, all artists have their causes. Maybe I'll be the guy to crusade against ring avulsions, although I'm not sure the issue will sustain a telethon. I could look up Eric Teanecker. He used to do the local news, so he's comfortable on TV. Maybe we could throw a little something together. Get some good slogans going. Let's see: "Take Your Ring Off Your Finger, Not Your Finger Off With Your Ring." "Don't Be An Idjit, Save Yer Digit." "Give Ring Avulsions the Finger."

Folks, I apologize. I've turned a perfectly lovely discussion into the aesthetic equivalent of the Texas Chainsaw Massacre, finger puppet version. I didn't see it coming either. But I'll stand tall and tell you what: I believe we saved some fingers today.

LOGGER CLOGS

I finally threw out my old plastic clogs the other day. They were cheapo knockoffs meant to emulate a certain recently very popular foam-rubbery clog made by a company for which I am not a financially remunerated spokesperson, so I won't utter the brand name aloud but let's just say it's short for "very much like an alligator but not an alligator." I can wait a second if you need me to. Also, times being tough and me being a free market sorta guy, let it be known I'll happily say the name right out loud if the company in question wishes to submit an offer. Baby needs new shoes, as it were.

It took me years to get my first pair of clogs because as a roughneck farmboy I still associated them with insidious counterculture, mysterious Dutch folk (the noble Hans Brinker excepted), and oddly cosmopolitan emergency room physicians imported from the East Coast. But then one day I went to visit my brother Jed—a farmer, a logger, and a *real* roughneck who once singlehandedly dragged himself from the woods after having his skull split by the butt-end of a flailing tree—and found him in his shop sharpening a man-sized chainsaw while wearing a pair of those rhymes-with-the-last-name-of-the-guy-who-founded-McDonald's clogs.

I found this freeing. Although I did not actually say to my brother, "I find this freeing!" as he was within easy reach of a canthook and two crowbars. Furthermore, although he has made a remarkable recovery in the wake of the logging accident, he did after all crack his cranium like a discount macadamia nut, and whether or not this has made him at all unstable it has left him with the perfect *excuse* for unstable behavior. Also, way back when he was toddling in soggy training pants he rapped our flu-ridden brother John right in the head with a hammer, as if disgusted by his weakness. I guess what I'm saying is, we love our brother Jed, but it doesn't hurt to keep one eye on the nearest exit.

Having seen my lumberjack brother thus shod, I was now prepared to hurdle my longstanding footwear prejudices—until I went to town and found out how much these things cost. Not crazy expensive, I guess, but just enough to give my hand pause en route to my wallet, during which pause I spotted a bin of what I shall call alterna-clogs. They lacked the trademark ventilation ports and heel strap, were the color of a dehiscent peach, and looked as if they had been molded from a vat of discarded putty, but they also looked like they would get a guy to the chicken coop and back, and what's more, they were four dollars.

That was around seven years ago. I figure those discount kicks amortized out to around fifty-seven cents a year. 'Course, the tread all wore off in the first few months, meaning during the winter I was a walking slip-and-fall and they are likely to blame for my one trick hip, and the liners rotted out years ago, and here lately if I fed the chickens after it rained, the chicken yard mud seeped up through the cracks in the soles, but all-in-all a pretty good run.

I'd probably still be running those old pasty heelless clod-hoppers except that my brother and sister-in-law recently gave me a pair of the real deals—the ones that are homophonic with the ceramic receptacle you store the butter in after you churn it. Having used the fake ones to get over my inhibitions, I just jumped right into the new ones. They're terrific.

So I'm going to visit my brother Jed again and tell him I'm just like him now. Except I've never gotten hit in the head by a tree.

RING ON, RING OFF

A few weeks back I somehow got to graphically rambling about injuries caused by wedding rings. I don't know how these things happen. I start out trying to be poetical about the nature of love and the beauty of human commitment and next thing I know I'm talking about degloving injuries and reconstructive hand surgery. One searches for the poetry only to be confronted with maceration and traumatic orthopedics. These are the sort of digressions that can be described as . . . well, if not career-ending, certainly career-deforming.

I wandered off into that whole tangent because I mentioned removing my wedding ring. What I meant to talk about was how although I'm a sentimentalist at heart, and very much in grownup love, I don't think it hurts to take your wedding ring off now and then. Some people are very superstitious on this point, and maybe I should be, but I'm not. I've been married almost nine years now, and when I pull the ring off and see the groove running the circumference of my finger, I like the idea that we got something going here that goes beyond jewelry. In the summer, when the absent gold reveals a slender band of white skin, I'm pleased that removing the ring fails to remove the evidence of the ring.

Not only am I not superstitious about pulling off the ring, I'm not even that picky about the ring itself. I've got two rings right now. The one I wear most often belonged to my wife's grandfather or great-uncle, we're not sure which. It was in a drawer in the farmhouse when we moved in. It's a little skinnier than I'd like, but then I've never operated at the cutting edge of taste or fashion. Plus, it gets the point across.

My other ring—my backup ring, the one I keep in the car in case I forget to take the main ring down off the pin before I hit the road—came from a head shop and cost nine dollars. It's one of those where if you don't like how it fits you can just squeeze it real hard and reshape it. Handy, eh? I bought the head shop ring to replace my original wedding ring, which was my step-father-in-law's wedding ring from his first marriage, proving among other things that I don't believe in bad karma when it comes to getting a wedding ring for free. I lost that original ring while delivering a breech lamb, and it is not outside the realm of possibility that it actually came off inside the sheep and resides there still. As an aside I can tell you that if you loudly declare that you lost your first wedding ring inside a sheep, you can get everyone in the bar to stop their beer halfway to their face, and you will have to leave before closing time.

Once I even had an earth mother friend give me a henna wedding ring. That was handy while it lasted.

The upshot is, I'm not particularly choosy about what sort of ring I wear—which is good, considering how fast I was going through them for a while there. In fact, as I tell you this story now I'm reminded that I lost yet another wedding ring in a fire truck. I removed it on my way to a fire so as to avoid hooking it on a hose rack and suffering the dreaded ring avulsion (the injury that got me off track the last time, and I promise not to go there again) and forgot to put it back on. Perhaps it rattles around the defroster still.

Ring on, ring off, it doesn't matter much to me, as long as the one who stood beside me the first day I wore it is still willing to stand beside me, no matter what sort of distractible meandering knucklehead I might be. You see, when I look at that ring, or the untanned indentation where the ring oughta be, I think, *lucky me, lucky me.*

WALKING NOWHERE

The other morning I got up and walked to work, and just kept walking. Now mind you, unless I'm out on the road peddling my charms and wares, I walk to work every day. It's a pretty straight-forward commute: out the front door, down the sidewalk, across the driveway, up a little rise around to the back of the garage, let myself in through the second-story door, and there y'are. (I won't count the trip out to the chicken coop and back because I'm trying to be modest.)

Although I have always remained relatively active and have never truly let myself go completely to flop, I have also spent a vast percentage of the last twenty-five years slumped in a chair at a keyboard or slumped behind the wheel of a car rolling to the next low-key whoop-de-doo. There have been certain doughy accumulations. Furthermore, one day not so long ago my brother the logger and I were comparing our accumulated clicks, twinges, and impingements and it struck me that apart from the fact that I have never been hit in the head with the butt end of a tree, he's no more physically frayed from his certifiably dangerous profession than I am from all my long-term butt parking.

Then the sitting studies started rolling in. Now, I'm a skeptic when it comes to popular medical news, since mostly what you get is the most superficial skimming of the most shocking scintillas, followed in five years by an utter reversal, and we all get nutritional whiplash as we trade out our low-fat margarine for stone-ground nut butters. I figure you get your genetics, you do basic due diligence, and then maybe you can tweak the remaining ten percent of fate. But these sitting studies made it sound like I might as well work in a burning tobacco factory as sit on my hinder from dusk to dawn, and—and this was the worst part—those intermittent jogs I was taking weren't enough to undo the sedentary bulk of the rest of the day.

And so I began to take preventive measures. First I tried sitting on a big red yoga ball. It was fine I suppose, but one day I got to bouncing on it as a form of procrastination and wound up knocking the computer monitor off the desk and injuring it well beyond the terms of the warranty. Next I tried a standing desk, but this only led to me slouching and slumping and leaning on my elbows the same as before only now while standing on my two flat feet. It was a minimal improvement at best.

Then my wife suggested I get a treadmill desk. I chuckled condescendingly, as she is ten years younger than me and thus surely lacks my capacity for skepticism, and never mind if she is really into high-level black-belt yoga and can do things like ski to the back forty and back, whereas I . . . I . . . aaand so I got a treadmill desk.

Do you know how hard it is to type *treadmill desk*? Of all the trend-chasing, fad-following silliness I've gotten myself involved in over time, this ranks right up there with parachute pants and jelly bracelets at the roller rink. Nothing like walking all day and getting nowhere. It's bad enough when the guys down to the feed mill ask me what I've been up to lately and I say, "Crafting precious metaphors." Now I have to say, "Crafting precious metaphors while walking 2.2 miles an hour—in place."

But you know what? Two months in I've dropped about fifteen pounds. Certain hitches in my giddyup remain, but I feel more spry in general. My record is eleven miles in one day, although it's usually more in the four- to six-mile range. I'll leave you with two final bits of information: the words you just read were written over the course of 3.85 miles, and whatever wisecracks you or the boys at the feed mill come up with, they're trumped in spades by the look in my wife's eyes when I come in the door after yet another nine-mile day at the office.

CHEATERS

The other day I was teaching my brother John about cheaters. It's not that we were thinking about becoming private investigators lurking in the lobby of the no-tell motel, it's that his eyes are beginning to fail him. This tickles me pink, because he is a sawyer, a pilot, a singer of barbershop harmonies, owner and operator of his own bulldozer, and head-to-head a much better shot with his deer rifle. Whereas I am a really good typer. So I jump at any chance to be the one educating him.

There is nothing dire afoot with my brother's eyeballs, just the standard early-forties fade, the one that's even harder to take for guys like us who have had better than 20/20 vision all our lives. Then comes the day when—at least this is how it happened with me—you raise your hand to clip your fingernails and they are oddly fuzzy. At first you fear some sort of creeping fungus, but then you tip your head back a tad and they come into clear focus and somewhere inside your internal you says, "Uh-oh."

A guy could go on, I suppose, about what a spiritual gully-washer this moment is, how those fuzzy fingernails represent the fraying of time and the very fading of life itself, but let's not get heavy; it's not like your liver dropped out on the sidewalk. Fact is, this is the sort of thing you can—pardon the pun—see coming. Plus, how many other mileage-based maladies can be cured for under three dollars, which is the upper-end price range for your low-end reading glasses, or, as we call them in our family: cheaters.

I gently informed my brother that his mortal depreciation will now be measured in increments of magnification. Based on my experience, I told him to start with the 1.25s but to keep a pair or two of 2.0s on hand for close-range detail work. Buy cheapo cheaters in bulk, I told him, and just sling 'em everywhere. I sow them to the six directions: my desk, the car, the bedside stand, the workbench down in the pole barn, the tackle box, the pockets of my hunting jackets and suitcases, beside the bathroom sink, and inside the little glove box on the tractor. Had I the funds and resources, I would hire a crop duster to scatter them over the farm in general.

A year ago our local rescue service was paged in the wee hours to help an elderly lady who was having cardiac symptoms. I was the first on scene. She was frightened and trembling as I took her vital signs. As I let the air out of the blood-pressure cuff and turned to read the dial, I suddenly realized that no matter how I squinted or tipped my head back, I couldn't see the number. It was the first time I realized my eyes could be a liability for someone else. After the woman was safely in the hands of paramedics and I returned home, the first thing I did was place two pair of reading glasses in my rescue kit. I have given my brother (we took our EMT training together twenty-five years ago) the same advice.

Mostly, though, I tell him about the good stuff. Like how the first time you peer over those lenses at some younger person, you feel suddenly wiser and summarily excused from all subsequent fashion trends. Or the joyful bonus of reaching up for your glasses to find not one but two pair on your head. And what an economical miracle it is, after squinting and scowling in a stubborn attempt to read the aspirin bottle, to pop on a pair of cheaters and find yourself glory-be hallelujah cured of your weak-eyed affliction. What a fabulous soul-shiner to rediscover words and letters that don't look as if they've been rolled in lint. Embrace the change, I told my brother, but only after donning your cheaters, so you don't accidentally hug the drill press.

GOZZLED

The other day my brother called to happily inform me that a grinding wheel he was using had exploded, with some of the shrapnel lacerating his neck not very far from several life-critical circulation points. Actually, what he said was, "Yah, it got me right in the gozzle." It turns out this was one of those cases where a quarter-inch or so either way made all the difference between a goofball phone conversation and a memorial service. But John wasn't shook up about it. In fact, we talked about that: about how when the universe decides to flick your ear instead of take your head off, the thing to do is to stop, direct your attention toward the powers that may be, nod your head and say, "So noted," and then get back to 'er. Or as my brother-in-law Mark would say, "Walk it off."

"Walk it off" is Mark's answer to pretty much everything. Hit your head on the truck hood? Walk it off. Burn your hand on a piece of welding? Walk it off. Wife ran off with the Schwan's man? Walk it off.

Where I come from there is a whole entertainment element to painful nonfatal mishaps. Once you determine that your buddy is still able to walk and talk after being hit in the head with a monkey wrench, nothing's funnier than seeing your buddy get hit in the head with a monkey wrench. Once while helping our neighbor Jerry unload silage wagons, I stood up directly beneath the silo chute and drove my cranium into the apparatus with a resounding thump. For half a second Jerry's eyes widened with concern; then as he saw I was still able to stand, he collapsed into giggles. This was a very kind and gentle man, but he just couldn't keep a straight face whenever someone got whacked.

Once he did get his. One of his milk cows became deathly and irretrievably ill and was in such discomfort that he asked my brother to come over with his deer rifle and mercifully dispatch it, which my brother did. Then they had to drag the giant corpse out of the barn. So my brother hooked a cable between the cow and the tractor and started slowly pulling the animal out. Somehow one of the cow's legs got caught on a stanchion and drawn way back. When the leg finally cleared the stanchion, the cow's hoof whipped around and smacked Jerry right in the kneecap. As he writhed and hopped around on one leg, my brother said, "You alright?" Jerry kept writhing and my brother patted his rifle. "'Cause I got one more shell . . ."

We all know of friends and family who have been subject to injuries that are not funny at all and in fact have been tragic. So I think the deal here is, whenever we can get away with laughing at the pain, we do. But we also try to incorporate a lesson from the pain, if our thick heads will allow it. When my brother called to tell me about the grinder explosion, he was sitting in his pickup in the Farm & Fleet parking lot. Said he was about to go in and purchase one of those—as he called it—"full-frontal" face masks. "Always thought they were kinda silly," he said, "but this has been a behavior-altering experience."

NO LIMITS

I woke up early this morning and moved the chickens to fresh grass, then drove to town and found myself caught in a traffic jam, which is to say there were three cars between me and the stop sign. This put me in a reflective mood, which was handy, because the vehicle ahead of me was fitted with a plastic license plate holder declaring, THERE ARE NO LIMITS.

I immediately started tallying up all evidence to the contrary.

First, foremost, and most problematic, there is a limit to my ability to believe there are no limits. This arises out of certain morose Scandinavian tendencies, festering curmudgeonry, frank peevishness, and a disappointing attempt at the high hurdles in 1982. Also, I was short on sleep and only twelve hours previous had been reviewing our auto insurance, both factors inimical to accepting the concept of there being no limits, even if it says so right there on the back of your RAV4 in all capital letters.

The last thing I want to do first thing in the morning is impugn the makers of motivational license plate holders, but: there are limits. There are limits to how I'm going to get anywhere stuck behind you at this stop sign. There are limits to my ability to do quadratic equations or choose correctly between *who* and *whom.* There are limits to how much ranch dressing you can get out of the bottle even after you leave it propped upside down for a week.

Getting more personally specific, my ability to grow hair on the topmost portion of my head is irrefutably limited, as is my ability to start a chainsaw on the first try without flooding it, to untangle fishing line without yanking on it, or to perform a grand jeté without a scissors lift and better health insurance. There is a scar above my left eyebrow that says my ability to levitate above concrete is fundamentally limited. Just up the road from here sits a banker with a calculator that proves my credit line is unequivocally limited.

My ability to impress my wife is limited, although within reasonable bounds, and she does give me do-overs.

There are limits to how much coffee you can drink before your eyelids quiver like hummingbird wings. There are limits to the number of cheese curds you can eat during a Packers game, although you'd be surprised. My patience is limited, especially with myself, especially when I do the same dumb things, over and over, again and again. In fact, in that context I could do with way more limits.

And under the category of modern heartbreak, there are limits to unlimited internet.

Just to prove I am open minded, I will entertain the idea that there are no limits to how long you can be put on hold while figuring out the limits to your unlimited internet, how far you can go without directions, or how deeply you can love a child.

The person who screwed the license plate holder to that car would say I've clearly and obstinately missed the point, and fair enough. What you have here is a person offering encouragement. Or, even better, exhortation. On any given Thursday morning we could all use a little exhortation. And maybe there was more to the message: THERE ARE NO LIMITS was printed across the top half of the plate holder, but the bottom half had snapped off, meaning I couldn't read the rest.

I found this limiting.

THE ROAD

Back home on the farm someone else is doing the chicken chores, because I've been on the road, and somewhere along the line on some ribbon of concrete a green mile marker flipped by and I thought, well, there's a metaphor on a stick, and I began to wonder just how many of those I've flashed past, and then it struck me that the more germane question would be how many *more* I'll flash past. This line of thinking caused me to hold the wheel a tad tighter, but it was a good sunny day and I had Townes Van Zandt on the CD player, so I couldn't maintain that level of grim focus, although in the moment it did occur to me that Townes was one of the too, too many we sadly file under Gone Too Soon, and I drove with two hands a few miles more.

When it comes to symbolic rumination, the road with a capital "R" is one of your top five metaphor generators, and it's easy, even when you are sliding along at just under seventy miles per hour with heated seats or chilled air, to construe that you are an explorer on the journey of a lifetime, because you are. Never mind that the journey does not cease just because you're at a stoplight. Metaphors are no fun if you stretch them too thin. No, it's more fun to think of ourselves on the move because that creates the impression that we are getting somewhere.

We are zipping along, though, and movement—movement of your own accord, I should say—is freedom made manifest. You really can't overstate that one, even if you're just popping over to the donut shop for coffee and a cruller. The world holds people by the millions who have never known the feeling of freewheeling. I try to remember this when I look up and see I still have half a day's drive ahead of me before I see the ones I love. I try to remind myself then that the intervening miles are not to be overcome but rather to be sailed. It's a blessing, the open road.

I used to spend a lot of time on the road with truckers, writing about their work and ways. My Uncle Stan was a trucker, and one of the few people for whom I still entertain the word *hero*. He took me across the country on eighteen wheels when I was a young man, and thus I gratefully blame his memory for the itch I feel when I'm on the back forty and hear the distant hollow howl of a set of doolies crossing the interstate rumble strip. Uncle Stan taught me to read the road; when you see a dark patch on the concrete, you watch for a bump just prior—the dark patch is caused by drops of oil jarred from the pans of thousands of vehicles as they hit that uneven spot. Not all of the road signs are mounted on posts. Some are laid right out there in the road for you to see, if you will only pay attention.

And now we're back to metaphor, which is fine, because if we can take a lesson from a thing, we should. And if we can turn sightseeing into insightseeing, well, that might make a little progress toward a better world. On the other hand, sometimes the best thing is to just let the road unroll, let the wheels carry you body and soul, let the miles flow around your head and through it, let those towns and those Townes songs cycle through, and rather than worry about fitting everything between square corners just roll and roll and roll on, knowing that the end of the road will arrive in its own fashion, in its own time.

PRIORITIES

Back home on the farm I've been running behind. That in and of itself isn't news—running behind is a way of life for me—but there is some waxing and waning, and lately it's been all waxing, and I'm not talking about reshaping my eyebrows, although based on recent trends toward mutant overgrowth I might add that to the list.

I'd like to point out that I'm not complaining about being "too busy," which has become the leading American form of humble-bragging reality avoidance and is usually more a reflection of privileged pursuits woven with a perversion of priorities than it is of overwork (and let the record show that I include myself in the allegation). But in this case I'm referring not to the "busyness" itself but rather the behavior that lands me there. Specifically, fits of manic optimism in which I resolve to write three books, a magazine article, and an album of original country music songs featuring the kazoo, split a winter's worth of wood, clean the granary, build the kids a clubhouse, mow the lawn, distill three pints of artisanal chive blossom vinegar, floss my diastema, pay the electric bill, plant cucumbers, take the kids fishing, write a love note to my wife, write a thank you note to my wife, locate the power steering leak, answer all red-flagged emails, adjust my deer stand, clean the gutters, take that one thing down to the pole barn, take those forty-seven things out of the pole barn, put eighteen new strings on three old guitars, replace the batteries in the headlamp I use to close the chicken coop door after dark, figure out why the guinea pig is acting so weird, figure out why I'm acting so weird, get those one-cent stamps to bring my postcard stamps up to speed after the latest rate hike, figure out why our internet is acting like it's powered by an off-kilter guinea pig, stack the wood I haven't split yet, read that one book in the stack of all the other books that got there because they were that one book I hadn't read yet, learn once and for all how to spell the word *privilege,* lubricate the treadmill, make more time to clean the gutters since I left it too long, churn the compost, finish that dealio I told that guy I'd do by Sunday, this being Saturday, call the bank to see that the check for the health insurance cleared, and, and, and . . .

Deep breath.

You know what's astounding about that list? It represents any given manic Monday. You know what's even more astounding? The fact that it takes me clear into Thursday before I realize: it ain't gonna happen. Because it never does. Never has. Not even close. Hope blooms eternal, despite all well-established evidence to the contrary. And so about twice a year I get fed up with all this random mental meandering and I become very firm with myself. I sit and I whittle everything down and I make a list. It's a ruthless process, and it yields a short, tight set of bullet points. No trivialities. No distractions. Lean and mean. From here on in, I really mean it, and I prove it by putting a headline above the bullet points—just one word, in all capital letters: PRIORITIES.

I just clicked over and had a look at the current all-capital PRIORITIES list. Thirty-six items. And that's not including any of the silly ones on the list I just shared with you.

I'm tired of running behind. It's time to buckle down. First order of business, keep the word PRIORITIES in all caps, but also underlined and in bold red. Yes. I'll add it to the list. Oh, and rotate the tires . . . and tack down that loose shingle . . . and . . .

REASONABLENESS

Back home on the farm the other day a fellow human being and I stood out in the wide open air and conversed at length on a difficult subject. The subject was not resolved, but that was never the expectation. Rather, we wound up marveling at the rare privilege of engaging in a discussion driven by neither rage nor rhetoric.

These days we are neck-deep in opinionators. The plumber is a pundit and your aunt is Tweeting talking points. 'Course, anytime I use the phrase "these days" I am revealing my own creeping codgerism, a condition encroaching on my soul at a rate corollary to the recession of my hairline. Fact is, vituperative verbal smackdowns are nothing new. Civil discourse has waxed and waned since Socrates took the hemlock, and you know you could always find some grump down at the end of the Athenian coffee bar who could snort into his macchiato and tell you that chowderhead Socrates was no Anaxagoras.

When I was a much younger man, my politics were firmly settled. My friend Gene's were settled exactly the opposite. We pelted each other with ideologic regurgitations, and when Gene moved away we continued to skirmish via photocopied news-letters, articles, and statistics highlighted and triple-underlined and (this being the pre-internet age) fired to-and-fro via the US Postal Service. It was a sweet coincidence then, when—each hav-ing composed a letter unbeknownst to the other—our terms of ceasefire crossed in the mail. Realizing we were at risk of killing our friendship with someone else's ammunition, we decided to put an end to the broadsides.

So often we find ourselves longing for nuance. For thoughtful exchange. For the chance to think out loud, take it back, and try again. I once received a very angry note from a man who said he was so torqued off by something I had written in a book that he threw it down immediately and would never read another word I wrote, which I take to mean he never got around to the part seven pages later where I retracted the passage that scorched his shorts in the first place.

I love my wife because on a regular basis she allows me to say the wrong thing, back up, reboot, and retry. She has this reasonableness about her. Proven in part by the fact that I once told her I loved her because of her reasonableness, and yet—having just received the complimentary equivalent of a vacuum cleaner for Christmas—she stayed with me.

At some point you have to make the call. Agreeing to disagree is by and large a theoretical privilege. And somebody has to lead the charge, speaking—or even braying—in the argot of attack and counterattack. To stir it up and take the flak. Was everyone a waffling muddler like me, no issue would be raised, no dragons slain. But we wafflers have a role too: to listen, absorb, chew things over, just stand there boots on the ground and hands in pockets, shooting the breeze and not each other.

Four hundred–plus years ago my favorite dead Frenchman, Montaigne, wrote that "harmony is a wholly tedious quality in conversation." In other words, there is more to be learned by knocking heads than nodding them in unison. But he didn't stick the word *conversation* in there by accident. He assumed we would convene in disagreement, but that we would indeed convene, and once convened would converse.

Eventually, back there on my farm, the man got in his pickup truck and drove away, and as I went about my chores I figured each of us had been convinced of maybe nothing save the value of humane exchange. We were staying with each other, working the corners and angles from all sides, trying for education over insinuation. Being reasonable.

Seems like a fine place to start.

PAST TENTS, PRESENT TENTS

Sometimes people ask how I get to the Big Top Chautauqua tent every weekend, especially in winter. Truth is, the tent is rolled and stashed in a shed from mid-September through early June; Mount Ashwabay is, after all, a ski hill in northern Wisconsin. And although the music is recorded live, my presence on the radio show is often accomplished via what I call "theater of the mind"—also known as the room above my garage.

But I do perform in person under the actual canvas several times each year and can conjure the feel of the tent in a trice, with just one line:

> *Welcome back to Tent Show Radio, folks, from the backstage dressing room with the one lonely little lightbulb burnin'* . . .

Just between you and me, there is more than one lonely little lightbulb back there. But when I'm trying to find the mood, I turn all those other lights off. I thrive in dimness. Draw your own conclusions.

FIRST TIME

In the book Truck: A Love Story, *I wrote about my first visit to Big Top Chautauqua. I trimmed it up and tamped it down and did it like this for the radio show.*

Welcome back to *Tent Show Radio,* folks, from the backstage dressing room with the one lonely little lightbulb burnin' . . .

I've been sitting here quietly during the break, using the solitude to make a little run down memory lane, back to the first time I ever came to the Big Top. Memory lane in this case is State Trunk Highway 13, more specifically the abbreviated terminal dogleg portion that runs east-west along the uppermost roostercomb of the good state of Wisconsin. I was in my faithful old Chevy Malibu, and there was a woman riding beside me, a woman possessed of various powers, the most pertinent of which to this day she transmits via a pair of blue eyes clear as sky and bright as diamonds. I didn't know it then, but I was a bachelor on my way to becoming not a bachelor.

We were driving like we were in love . . . lazing along, holding hands, breaking eye contact just long enough so I could negotiate the curves and swerve around tourists and turtles. It's a good drive for lovers, that eastbound stretch of 13. You've got the southern shore of Gitche Gumee right there at your driver's side elbow. Some days the water is incandescent blue and hopeful, other days it looks all steel gray and ship-sinky. On the gray days you'll want to roll that window down so you can feel the bite of the wind and then—for the full effect—cue up some Gordon Lightfoot. Out of respect, you are not allowed to roll the window back up until "The Wreck of the Edmund Fitzgerald" is fully concluded.

Port Wing. Herbster. We made our way, the distance between Highway 13 and the Great Lake waxing and waning until we stopped for smoked fish and a used book about Lenny Bruce from a shop in Cornucopia. We ate the fish shoreside, and the wind was a cold scour, but we sat close, and among other things, love is Sterno. In short, I was a goner, and by the time we hit the curl at Red Cliff that drops you down to Bayfield I was prepared to complete the necessary paperwork, and said so.

The woman in question informed me that we had known each other only three months and she would make her decision only after conducting a performance review at the six-month mark. That, I said at the time, was a rolled-up newspaper to the snoot.

By sunset, however, we had made our way to Mount Ashwabay, and I shall never forget the sight of this tent, a blue burst against the surrounding green, looking from a distance like a squat storybook caterpillar with its stripes of pearl gray. We got there early enough to sit in the grass and watch the crowd filter in, and it really is something to see them gather, everybody milling but quietly so, folks passing in and out of the tent and clusters of friends meeting up to have beers in the grass or eat bratwurst in the concession tent. As the light faded, the crowd gathered and turned itself inward, as if the people were metal filings and the big tent—lit from within now by bare bulbs strung through the quarter poles—was an electromagnet on a rheostat. We allowed ourselves to be drawn in as well. Then the house lights went down, the stage lights came up, and when, three months later, the woman with the blue eyes said for better or worse she too was willing to fill out the paperwork, well, I knew that our night in the Big Top had something to do with it.

FROM THE TOP

You hear that? The crowd has returned. I wonder if somebody out there is sitting beside some other body, wondering if they too might find love beneath the canvas. It happens, you bet. So as the lights come down, go on and pull that somebody special a tad closer and let the music and the canvas do the rest . . .

TAKING THE AIR

Welcome back to *Tent Show Radio,* folks. The audience is return-
ing from intermission after having had an opportunity—as they
used to say in grander days—to "take the air." No better place
to take the air, really, than up here on the open face of Mount
Ashwabay. This is enhanced air; air that has been scrubbed by
Lake Superior breezes, filtered for freshness through stands of
pine and poplar, and infused with the sound of song. I dare say
this is edifying air, air that stimulates your cultural and intellec-
tual improvement. Goodness knows I can stand a few lungfuls.
If I were the kind of guy to hire a life coach—well, first of all I'd
have to hire six, and they'd have to take shifts. Even then they'd
all probably just knock off early and hit the bar to gorge on pick-
led eggs and do Jäger bombs in a desperate attempt to repress
everything as quickly as possible.

If I did hire a life coach, I would request specific guidance
in the area of edification. I have tried the self-edification route,
but I never quite seem to get through it without finding a wad
of figurative spinach stuck in my all-too-literal teeth. One time I
read a *New Yorker* article about the Ring Cycle and got all fired up
about the potential operatic acculturation and ordered a Wagner
CD, only to find out when it arrived that I'd picked the one with
the helicopters from *Apocalypse Now* on the cover. Another time
I resolved to comprehend jazz. I read a book about John Coltrane
and then put on one of his albums while I worked. I admit I was
probably a little distracted and probably had been eating too

44

many Little Debbie Zebra Cakes, but at some point my attention swung back to the music and I heard, ". . . a love supreme . . . a love supreme . . . a love supreme . . ."

"A-ha!" I thought. "I am beginning to understand! He is building on a repetitive theme!" I felt a surge of pride. I understood jazz! Another forty-five minutes would pass before I realized I had the CD player on single-song repeat and had listened to the same track thirty-seven times straight.

Once—mostly, I admit, in the service of love—I tried to learn French. I mastered two phrases. The first was *Est-que les vaches sont dans l'étable?* "Are the cows in the barn?" I cannot begin to explain the situation that precipitated that particular interrogatory. Naturally, the second phrase I learned was *Je nes palpa français,* which as far as I know is French for "I don't understand French." If that's not what it means, please don't tell me.

My wife is fluent in Spanish. I have one brother-in-law from Ecuador and another from Panama. Most of the family (children included) is bilingual on a sliding scale from fluent to . . . me. Thus, at our get-togethers I have the opportunity to polish my Spanish. Mainly what I've learned is that when it comes to raising children, you really need only two words in Spanish. The first is *cuidado,* which basically means "be careful." The second is *despacio,* which very loosely translated means "for the love of Pete, take it down a notch!" So when you find yourself in charge of a backyard full of screaming bilingual kids, you just stand there hollering, "Cuidado! Despacio! Cuidado! Despacio! DESPACIO!"

When you blend a family of native Central and South Americans plus Scandinavian cheeseheads, you get what I call your Scandihoovian Spanglish. Just the other day my toddler was doing something mildly dangerous and I found myself saying, "Cuidado, 'dere!"

She knew exactly what I meant.

Bottom line is, I'm the kind of guy who's happy to attend the opera, but I should like to be allowed to wear steel-toed boots with my evening suit. I like to read *Harper's* with a chaser of *Var-*

mint Hunter Magazine. Maybe that's why I enjoy a good show under canvas. Here we sit, brain-deep in arts and culture, but we're also just people hanging out in a tent, some of us wearing boots, a few of us wearing Birkenstocks, and best of all we're breathing free fresh air filled with music.

SWEATY CHEESE AND INJURED CEREAL

One of my favorite things about the tent shows is the sound of guests at intermission. It's a gentle sound. It's a warmhearted sound. It's the sound of old friends reuniting and strangers getting along. It's the sound of people visiting.

You know what? It's the sound of happiness.

And why not? Here we are, feet planted right on the earth. It really is a tent, you know. No floorboards. You come to the Big Top, your feet remain in contact with the planet. You'll catch the light scent of gently trampled grass (yah, you can trample something gently, it just takes time and civilized persistence), you'll hear the crunch of gravel underfoot, a whisper of canvas on canvas, and now and then when the wind is right you'll catch a whiff of bratwurst sizzling under the food tent across the way. And you can eat a brat when you're up here with no worries because the rest of the experience is so very heart-healthy.

Me, I'm backstage picking around what's left over on the deli tray. It starts out as a nice little spread, as well it should be: hungry musicians are cranky musicians, and cranky musicians tend to slide off key or transpose everything into the key of D-minor, the saddest of all keys.

But now there's not a lot left of that deli tray—just three pieces of sweaty cheese. No surprise, really. I spent some of my formative years in the company of country music roadies, and they taught me the two most important rules of the road (and life). Number One, if you get ten minutes, sleep. Number Two, if you see food, eat it.

I always kinda operated that way anyway, at least on the food front. I was raised in a big farm family. When we had company for dinner, before passing the first bowl of food Dad used to tell the guests, "Take what you want the first time, because it ain't comin' around again." Mom fed us mostly on oatmeal out of a twenty-five-pound bag. One fall she got a garbage pail full of wheat from the neighbor's gravity box grain wagon, and for a pretty long stretch there we had boiled wheat for breakfast. The only time we got box cereal (which we called *boughten* cereal because, well, because it *didn't come from the neighbors' gravity box*) was on Sunday mornings, because Mom had to get six or eight kids ready for church and she didn't have time to boil all that wheat. And even then she bought all the box cereal at some big ol' scratch-and-dent warehouse up a back alley somewheres.* We used to say we never ate a box of cereal that hadn't been backed over by the truck that brought it. I guess you could have called it injured cereal. But compared to a vat of oatmeal, that injured cereal was pretty good stuff. I remember one time my brother and I were watching TV at my grandma's and that Total cereal ad came on, the one where they stack up twelve bowls of Froot Loops next to one bowl of Total and the announcer says, "You'd have to eat twelve bowls of Froot Loops to equal the nutrition in one bowl of Total." My brother looked at me and said, "I'll take the twelve bowls of Froot Loops."

Anyways. I have no complaints about the deli tray, although I do have to say that seeing this is Wisconsin, next time would it kill 'em to throw in a little lefse? I'm gonna have my people talk to their people.

*Yep, I know: "somewheres." Was gonna change it for the book, but that's how we say it where I'm from. Especially when we're feeling comfortable. See also: "Youse guys" and "Anyways . . ."

A WORLD AWAY

When I was a little boy, maybe four or five years old, Grandma got us a tent. We pitched it in the front yard, and I still carry a vivid memory of the separate world that tent created. A world that smelled of tromped grass and stale sunlight. A world that made my little liver quiver as I imagined myself an explorer lost somewhere in the land of Tarzan even though Mom and pancakes were just forty feet away. Maybe that was the best part about a tent: it created a world away.

I was raised in a fundamentalist Christian sect. I like to say that because it makes people pull up short—they think I was raised inside a walled compound where we hoarded diesel fuel and fertilizer. (We actually did hoard diesel fuel and fertilizer, but we used them to raise corn.) Part of being in this church was that we didn't actually have churches; we met for Sunday morning meeting in regular houses except for the time once a year when we met for what we called convention. For convention we came from all over the state and convened on a farm, where we parked our cars in the hayfield and held services in an old barn. Our hymns rose through the rafters of the haymow. When it was time to eat we'd head across the grounds to a big old army surplus tent. We gathered outside the flap and waited. When everyone was ready, the dinner bell rang and someone pulled back the flap. We filed in quietly and found our place in long rows of tables and benches. The silverware was wrapped in a napkin and all of the cups and dishes were upside down, I suppose for sanitary reasons. We sat in silence. Part of the reason we were quiet is because we were churchly, but there is also something in the nature of a tent that is conducive to quietness and reflection—it's the scent of the earth and the grass but it's also the enveloping canvas that shelters you and dampens and tempers any noise that does arise. So we'd sit there quietly and then a sister minister would lead us in singing grace. When we hit the final note there was a grand clatter of cutlery and porcelain and coffee mugs being flipped over and the tent would soon fill with the aroma of what we called convention stew, which was your basic hearty beef-and-vegetable stew made in a tureen the size of a washing machine.

Not all of my tent memories are so heart-warming. When I was still a tot, Mom took me to the circus. About halfway through the production a clown began soliciting audience volunteers for his act. I scrunched down next to Mom but he homed right in on me. Plucking me out of the crowd, he stood me in the center ring. I could feel the heat of the lights as he spoke into his microphone.

"What's your name, little boy?"

"Mike," I whispered.

"Oh, you're going to have to talk louder than that," said the clown. "What's your name?"

"Mike," I squeaked. All this time the clown was keeping the microphone to himself.

"Oh, no, you gotta be a *lot* louder than that," he said again. "Just yell your name right out so people can hear you!" And right when I yelled "Mike!" he jammed the microphone into my face and I was shocked to hear my little voice reverberating throughout the gigantic tent.

The clown then proceeded to conduct a number of humiliating bits that culminated in him tipping me over his knee with my butt pointed toward the bleachers. He dusted my little hinder with a gigantic pink feather duster, then reached into the waistband of my pants and through some sleight of hand pulled out a huge pair of baggy women's underwear. The audience roared.

Finally he carried me back and released me to Mom. "You're a good little sport," he said. "I want to give you something to remember this day by." (As if I would have problems remembering this day, I'm thinking, still freaking out forty years later.) He pulled out a balloon and blew it up until it was longer than I was tall. With the spotlight still on us, he handed it to me." Here y'go, little feller," he said, and as I reached for it he let go and it went farting off into the air, corkscrewing into flaccidity and nothingness while once again the audience roared.

So you'll understand that among the many reasons I enjoy coming up to Big Top Chautauqua is because it's always a world away, and with each visit I'm pretty much guaranteed a few new canvas-scented memories.

But best of all? Zero sociopathic clowns.

FLYING ABOVE THE CANVAS

The guest for this show was Paul LaRoche, performing with Brulé and AIRO. LaRoche honors his heritage by singing of the people, land, and history of the Lower Brule Sioux Reservation of South Dakota, and the performance I refer to here included dancers in traditional regalia. That said, LaRoche will be the first to tell you that his music draws on more than one world and in fact draws on the seven directions.

Earlier tonight during the show, when the drums were pounding and the dancers were spinning and the flute was swirling, I took myself out of the tent and imagined myself high in the sky above Mount Ashwabay—perhaps on manmade wings of silver, perhaps on feathers alone—and as the final few minutes of sunlight hit the sloped face of the earth, there far below I saw the still, blue dot of this tent, surrounded by thousands of acres of quiet twilit forest, and thinking of the power and color and life pulsing at the center of that blue dot I marveled again at the idea of what transpires as a result of the simple act of creating a space. A space aside: aside from the hustle, aside from the grind, aside from the things we have grown used to. Aside from the well-worn grooves. A place where, even if the music is thunderous, we are allowed the gift—so rare in our pandemonious world—of reflection. The gift of time and place aplenty to turn yourself over to the sound and spirit and see where you are flown. Tonight, after only a few heartbeats of music, I felt thunderstorms approaching across a broad plain, I felt a western river valley open before me, I felt the call of a people through time. I heard ghosts marching.

Day-to-day, I'm pretty much boots and blue jeans. Pork chops and pickup trucks. Can't dance a lick, and don't care to. Not inclined to carry on. But I learned a long time ago there is value now and then in turning yourself over to the moment. To letting your soul wander out there unprotected. Oddly enough—or not oddly at all, if you give it proper consideration—much of my openness to this idea comes as a result of my being raised in a fundamentalist faith. I learned at an early age what it is to turn yourself over to a greater mysterious power and sign off on the idea that things are bigger than you and that there is more to life than just puttin' on a big pair of boots and stompin' around. I wandered other paths in the years that followed, and generally prefer pondering to preaching, but I have never lost the thread of the idea that it is in those moments when we let our hearts fly right out of our chests that we are closest to understanding the mystery of our clunky lives on this earth. Or if not understanding the mystery, understanding each other. We are all related, says Paul LaRoche.

Whether they emanate from the Bible on my lap at a gospel meeting in a bank basement or from a Native American flute, those things in the air that we cannot touch, that we cannot grasp, are nonetheless the things that can lift us above every earthbound worry. At times tonight I can feel the flow of long-gone buffalo, and I yearn for the idea of prairies before man—any man—and in that yearning is something even a lapsed, post-Calvinist Scandihoovian knucklehead can recognize as transcendent and universal, something between this time and time past, and I wonder as I hear the flute whipping like a prehistoric wind if perhaps that is the most universal human longing of all—the longing for the beginning of everything, for a clean slate and a fresh soul, for a fresh humanity. What is the sound of a flute, after all, but human breath dancing?

We will leave this tent soon enough. The clunky day-to-day awaits. Boots on the ground, pickup truck to the feed mill.

But for just a little while longer, I would like to fly.

BLACK DOG

Welcome back to *Tent Show Radio,* folks, from the backstage dressing room with the one lonely little lightbulb burnin'. . .

Back home on the farm I just came off a little stretch where I was feeling glum. Nothing big, no need for cards and letters, doin' fine, just one of those deals. For reasons that I've previously classified as biochemical, genetical, banal, and foolish in the face of good fortune, I have off and on throughout this life found myself in the company of what Winston Churchill called—at least I think it was Winston, and I'm going with that even if it's wrong just to spite Google by not doing the instant cellphone search that has come to replace our carbon-based brain cells—"the black dog." Now my black dog is hardly worth talking about, really. I've had friends and acquaintance whose black dogs gnawed right through their breastbone and into their vitals and in some cases ate them alive. My black dog is smallish and nibbles at my belly button now and then, or walks in all wet and shakes cold swampwater on my toes, but within a day or two or a week at most, it wanders off to hide behind the barn and I can feel the sunshine again.

I don't mind that little black dog, because he tends to direct my eyeballs inward. Not just to gaze at my navel, but deeper, into the darker corners of those mysterious inward shadowy elements of ourselves we can't really describe or put a location on but we feel with the very same heaviness as if they were clearly labeled on page 37 of some anatomy textbook somewhere. It's good, I think, for me to look in the acorporeal mirror and see nothing looking back and wonder what's missing, or what needs sunlight. Some of the best progress I've made as a human being has come when I was brought low enough to consider the worst I might be as a human being. Wasn't any fun, but one hopes it pays off in the long run.

Clearly these ramblings require a disclaimer. The real black dog—the big, lurking, foul-breathed drooler—is no help at all. It is one thing to feel a little down; it is another to feel utterly out. I do have a nursing degree and once spent time answering a suicide hotline, so you understand I don't intend to minimize the real deal. Some battles are not meant to be fought in the dark alone. Don't do it. Don't let your friends do it. But as for me and my generally trainable black dog, I've learned to live with him, and as long as he's around, rather than let him back me into a corner I try to follow him someplace useful.

And it's funny what will run him off. Usually it's just time. In other cases the change is so abrupt it's clear some intracellular switch got knocked back into the "function" position. And sometimes exterior forces will do the trick. Like, oh, say, gathering in a big happy tent with other happy humans. Sometimes a physical remove delivers a psychological remove—it may not even last, but for a little while your brain gets pointed in another direction and your heart beats to a more lively rhythm. Maybe church will do it for you, or maybe a group of friends telling old stories around a kitchen table, or maybe just a road trip to an unfamiliar city. I can tell you I've shown up at this tent more than once with the black dog riding in the back seat, and then I'll be in here and the music will be going and the people will be rocking or swaying or applauding or just sitting quietly with their faces tilted toward the stage just so, and I'll look around and hey—no black dog. He may be waiting in the car, he may jump out from the ditch somewhere along the road home, but he for dang sure ain't gettin' in this tent.

So I look forward to the second half of the show here, listening to music that is to black dogs what that mail carrier spray bottle is to nippy-yippy dogs. It's nice just to get together and feel the sunshine, even if you are under a tent after dark.

Oh, and P.S.: I may have made up the word acorporeal *also but am maintaining my Google holiday and will not look it up until the show is over.*

CANVAS RAIN

During this performance we could hear the sound of rain hitting the tent. It was lovely.

Did you hear the rain on the canvas earlier? That was nice, I thought. The thing about music in a tent is, as long as everything's battened down and buttoned up, the rain can be part of the show without wrecking the show. The click and the trickle, the tappety-tap, the steady fall of it, it's a soft carpet of sound that only adds to the coziness of the space. Outside of blizzard nights, never does our old farmhouse feel so safe and gracious as when I am tucking my daughters abed and through the hip roof just feet above us we can hear the muffled finger-drumming of rain on the shingles.

Rain can run you right out of adjectives. It falls an infinity of ways, it sounds an infinity more. Tonight the rain is striking canvas stretched tight as a drumhead, so every little drop lands with a percussive splat. It is the sound of leprechauns applauding.

Rain on a flat rock sounds different than rain on a round rock. Rain on green leaves sounds different than rain on fallen leaves. Rain on your picnic table sounds different than rain blown sideways against a window. Rain on an umbrella sounds different than rain striking the bottom of an upturned canoe.

The sound of rain is colored by your circumstance: the sound of rain on a cold day versus the sound of rain on a warm day; the sound of rain on withered corn versus the sound of rain for the seventh day straight; the sound of rain when you are standing in dry socks versus wet socks.

When I worked on a hay crew in Wyoming, the sound of rain on the bunkhouse roof in the morning meant I'd be trading my swather and the wide-open spaces for a paintbrush in the boss's wife's kitchen. Earlier in the season, when I was working on the irrigation crew, rain in the morning just meant I'd be wet all day.

Twenty years after I dug my last feeder ditch, my boss contracted cancer and I returned to the ranch to do the job again. He was a hero of mine and responsible for some of the few threads of good character I might possess. The day before he left for the hospital, we were working the big ditch up top and a ferocious rain blew in. We ran for the pickup truck and talked over the roar of the storm. My wife and I were only recently married; he and his wife had grown children. "Your wife," he said. "She's a good woman." The rain rattled on, and he grinned a little. "You and me," he said, "we both did better than we deserved." It was as close a moment as we ever shared, and I'm not sure it ever would have happened had the rain not driven us into the cab of that truck.

Rain is a sight as well as a sound. Think of a dry stretch, and then the first fat drops pockmarking the dust. Think of raindrops curving through a headlight's beam. Think of the streetlight rainbow slicks as the first rains raise the oil from the asphalt.

During a recent stretch of drought, clouds would appear in the hot afternoon, small and scattered as spooked sheep, and here and there thin gray streamers of rain would drape down, then seem to evaporate before hitting the ground. My brother the farmer swore the streamers would veer away from his plowed fields, perhaps brushed aside by the heat rising from the baked earth.

"I love a rainy night," sang Eddie Rabbitt back in the '80s, and the people agreed, sending the song to number one on both the pop and country charts. Rabbitt understood the power of precipitation. In another of his number ones, he sang about driving on a rainy night with "those windshield wipers/slappin' out a tempo/ keepin' perfect rhythm/with the song on the radio . . ." Above all, rain is rhythm. A perfect match for music.

Hear that? Rain stopped. It's good, I suppose. The last few folks are making their way back from the concession tent for the second act, and they won't have to hike their windbreakers up over their heads or run, on the theory that fewer raindrops strike a moving target. But I'll miss the rhythm a little bit, the sound of those tiny leprechaun hands clapping. Into each life some rain must fall and then stop falling.

THE INNER CIRCLE

The one thing cozier than a tent? Home—and those who make it so.

SONG FOR MY DAUGHTERS

The first time Brandi Carlile came to the Big Top tent, she was playing solo and opening for the Indigo Girls. For the show surrounding this monologue, she was headlining with her own band and the place was packed from canvas wall to canvas wall with fans she earned song by song, going way back to the days when she was recording music on her own time and her own dime. Brandi Carlile's music is built first of all on lyrics that read like true American poetry . . . poetry of the road, poetry of universal human connection, and, once she's got you well in for the ride, poetry for stomping yer boots. Above all, though, it is Brandi Carlile's voice you'll take with you. Her voice, and how she inhabits it. Rarely have power and vulnerability so naturally melded. It is as if the heart of a sparrow has been wrapped in brass. When Brandi Carlile sings, she can belt it or she can break it, but above all she can bring it.

I have two daughters. So including my wife, at my house it's three-to-one girls against boys. A fellow I met recently on the road told me, "You don't have a family, you have a sorority."

I think before I was a dad I would have appreciated Brandi Carlile simply for her music. For her art. But as a father of two girls, I appreciate Brandi Carlile far beyond her lyrics and melodies. When I hear her sing out strong, even when her voice breaks, I think of my girls growing older, and I'm glad they live in a time when there are Brandi Carliles from whom they may seek some guidance.

I mean, Dad will do his best, and Mom (the woman I used to refer to as my wife, until the time my actual mom became Grandma and my wife became Mom—those of you out there with tots of your own will understand) is a woman of strength and virtue and qualified discretion (I say qualified discretion because despite strong evidence of her own good character she married me, which seems a bit of a theoretical chink in the ol' armor), so we'll do what we can, but no matter how parents try there are those gaps and unforeseen developments in which outside influence—for better or worse—will fill the empty space. Good to know Brandi Carlile is an option.

I was thinking about my daughters during a song Miss Carlile sings with the lyrics that go:

> There are miles of hay like I have never seen
> Just when you think you've had enough and
> Your dreams come true
> I just want to be closer to you . . .

I spend eighty to a hundred days a year on the road telling stories or singing songs or sometimes both. It's a blessing, this life. Better than I might have hoped or deserved. And the road is not a hardship. I was raised by and around truckers gone every week. And many of our neighbors and relatives are in the military. When I speak with my daughters about my absences, for purposes of calibration we always refer to cousin Steve, currently scheduled for his fourth deployment, and him with a wife and toddlers.

So one never wants to get too dramatic. Especially in my case, in which more often than not this thing I call "The Road" is within a half-day's drive of my chicken coop. But of course you think of your children and wonder what is learned in your absence. Or by your absence. I think sometimes, while I'm driving through the night alone, of what or whom I want my daughters to know, or believe . . . what I would tell them if they were in the passenger seat.

First thing: Your dad was in over his head. Constantly, and in all respects. My learning curve often lagged behind my balding curve.

I would tell them to beware youthful boys and dissolute men, who are knuckleheaded and inept in every respect except for the ability to worm their way into a young girl's heart.

I would tell them to run close to the ground because eventually we all fall.

I would tell them to get a good pair of boots. Today's woman should own a good pair of boots. (Ones that lace up and last, and steel toes are never a bad idea.)

I would tell them to leave affectionate notes for their mother as I do, but with greater frequency than I have. I would tell them that once a week they should offer their mother a blanket apology for everything in general. That one I'm pretty regular with.

I would tell them to strive for charity, and I'm not just talking about dropping a nickel in the can or boxing up your old socks.

I would tell them to doubt anyone who speaks with absolute authority. Rather, I would tell them to go to the ridge at midnight and stare into the stars for five minutes. Accept infinity, and humility follows.

I would tell them, never smoke cigarettes, but if a pleasing puff of pipe smoke drifts your way, take a whiff. This guards against prudery and furthermore there are times in the face of pleasure when we should do the obvious.

And, after what I've heard tonight, I would tell them, daughters, when the time is right and you're on your own, take to the open road yourself, and whether that road is in your soul or out your windshield, drop the hammer and run it with open heart, open eyes, and open ears. Check the mirror for your old dad now and then. He'll do his best, but he knows the time is coming when you will chase the sunrise on your own.

PET OF THE WEEK

My elder daughter sat down at the supper table the other night and announced that for her school service project this semester she has decided to volunteer at the local humane association. Naturally I am pleased that she has chosen to combine scholarship and civic-mindedness. I am also pleased because my dear departed grandmother was instrumental in establishing the local humane association and even got my grandfather to serve on the board for a time, although he always skipped the November meeting to go deer hunting, an absence that caused some consternation among the elderly female bridge-playing members of the board, but Grandpa was a salesman by nature and trade, and by the time the money was counted from the gigantic raffle he orchestrated each January, all was forgiven.

Every summer when I was in grade school, my brother John and I would leave the farm to spend a week at Grandma's house in the city. Every morning she fed us Apple Jacks and white toast with grape jelly, then loaded us into her orange Plymouth Duster and drove us out to the animal shelter, where we cleaned cages and changed food bowls and took the dogs for walks. We also hung out with the shelter employees, several of whom were dedicating their lives to helping the animals as a result of the terms of their probation, and by the time work was over my brother and I were conversant in the intricacies of Huber law and work release privileges. One summer we worked with a high-strung smoker named Randy. Too young to understand the power of addiction, we thought it would be a real hoot to hide his cigarettes. After a two-hour stretch in which he grew more and more agitated and eventually began to tremble like a juiced hummingbird, we snuck the cigs back into the break room where he could find them. He pounced on the pack, lit up immediately, and took a drag so deep he nearly rose out of his socks. Then, on the exhale, he uttered what even to my young ears was the most comically contradictory phrase ever: "Oh . . . that's just like a breath of fresh air!"

Each week the local newspaper sent a photographer to the shelter to get a mugshot of some cat or dog that would then be featured in that week's edition under the heading "Pet of the Week." When my brother and I were visiting, Grandma always made us cradle an animal each and be included in the photograph. I'm sure her heart was in the right place, but putting your grandkids in the paper under the heading "Pet of the Week" really sets them up for some introspection over time. I submit for a fact that my brother still ain't right.

These days underage volunteers must be accompanied by an adult, so I'll be taking a few shifts with Amy. I accompanied her on the orientation tour. Naturally there have been a host of changes at the shelter since my brother and I were perambulating the poodles and hanging out with hollow-eyed smokers on parole, but as so often happens, the smells and sounds took me right back to those days decades back. Those cats and dogs need a new generation of caretakers. My daughter has a great capacity for kindness, and I hope this experience will expand that capacity, although based on the look in her eyes as we took our orientation tour, I'd better start budgeting for doghouse lumber. Perhaps this won't turn so much into an exercise in kindness and civic-mindedness as an exercise in me holding the line: last week, after her first day of volunteering, my daughter leapt out of the van and ran toward me. "Ferrets!" she said, joyfully. "They have ferrets!"

The road is long, my friends.

DUMPSTER DATE

My wife has been pricing dumpsters. The big ones. The ones that arrive on their own flatbed truck.

I'd like to think I'm not a hoarder, but if you ask my wife I'm just a few *National Geographic* stacks short of certifiable. I justify all the boxing up and piling up with the fact that I generate most of my lunch money by writing stories, and you just never know when—for the sake of veritas—you're gonna need the fake parking ticket your buddy used to prank you back in 1988, so you cram it in a banker's box along with all those receipts for the economy size barrels of hair conditioner you were buying in 1988 because you fancied yourself quite the Midwestern Fabio and the pending follicular recession was only a faint gleam in your well-used mirror.

Time passes. Your hair falls out. You get married. Your wife is an eminently reasonable woman, so when she hints maybe you could get rid of some those boxes mouldering in the rafters of the garage you give it fair consideration, but then one day you're working on a book about your old truck and you want to tell the story of the fake parking ticket, and because you are blessed with a Midwestern work ethic and a healthy dose of OCD, you spend the better part of an afternoon sweating and bumping your bald head up there in the rafters, all hunched over and riffling through vintage dentist appointment reminders until—Victory!—three hours later you find the fake parking ticket and the story winds up in the book and that justifies every last box in the garage, even the one containing flat racquetballs and rusty roller skates.

Then you are hired to compose a video essay based on the state of your garage and you pull out the bag of shoes you've been collecting since you were a freshman in high school and as you describe how fleet of foot this mouse-gnawed New Balance racing flat made you back in the days before you were dragging around all your bad habits, you realize this is not junk, this is a goldmine, a repository of fungible history that can theoretically be converted into health insurance premiums, and so you move the cars out of the garage for good and continue to accumulate accumulations.

But then you move to a farm, and instead of one garage, you now have one garage and two pole barns. Two BIG honkin' pole barns. Those pole barns are nothing fancy, but they are vastly capacious, and now with all that extra room not only do I expand my—ahem—archives, I also find it perfectly natural to spend the afternoon dumpster diving for bricks at a construction site, or trucking home a giant stack of vintage insulation, or adding to my collection of distressed windowpanes, or taking delivery of thirty-seven plastic pails that smell like pickles.

This week there was a family meeting. My wife. Me. And a calendar. Upon which five days in June are now highlighted and labeled DUMPSTER WEEK.

At our house, my wife is in charge of reality, so I'm going along with the plan. I did broach the idea of "fungible history," but the look I received in return implied that if I kept it up one day I would step through the pole barn door and find myself greeted by fifteen concerned family members and a television crew.

In a preemptive move designed to steel myself against the arrival of the dread dumpster, I have been polishing up a few of my most precious possessions and offering them for sale on Craigslist and eBay, which leads me to ask: how many gallons of Febreze are required to obscure the scent of mouse pee permeating four pickup loads of used insulation?

CHICKEN COOP CAMPOUT

Last week I wound up sleeping in our brand new chicken coop, which at first might sound as if it's going to be a tale of marital woe, but thankfully this is not the case. No, this is a story about being a dad, or trying to be a dad.

I got a late start in that department, meeting my elder daughter—my given daughter, as I call her—when she was three and I was in my late thirties. Amy has proceeded to light up my life in ways I did not anticipate. Of course she has also thrown me into the bottomless pits of uncertainty, as that is what children do to grownups who think they have it all figured out. You just never know if you're doing the right thing or not. Shortly after we met I taught her to perform pantomime dog tricks. That is, I would tell her to sit and she would sit. I would tell her to roll over and she would roll over. I would throw her an imaginary dog treat and she would catch it. In between she would pant happily, her tongue out and waggling. The show really got to be pretty popular with the relatives and, frankly, pretty much anyone who would stand still for it, and we even worked up this bit where I would veeerrry carefully place an imaginary dog treat on her nose, then say, "Staayyy . . . staayy," and then I'd snap my fingers and she would flip the imaginary treat into the air and catch it on the way down. We were doing this in the living room one day and folks were applauding and Amy was wagging her pretend tail and suddenly it hit me that the day she finally dials up social services, this little bit right here will be number one on the list of submitted indignities.

Amy stopped doing the dog tricks a few years ago. She's already nearly as tall as me and on the verge of becoming a young lady. And this is the other thing about children: at some point after they stop howling all night and toothlessly gnawing on your chin, they learn to walk, and once they learn to walk they find their way to the clock of time and attach a rocket to the minute hand. I find myself breathless sometimes when I look at my children and want desperately to slow things down. When my younger daughter, Jane, became potty-trained, the only drawback was that she couldn't reach the bathroom light switch, so Dad still had to lever his lard out of the chair whenever she went in there. Then our friend Lori made her a flat stick with a scallop and a hole in one end. By using the scallop to push the switch up and the hole to pull the switch off, Jane could run the light herself, and Dad could remain a lump. Then one day Jane called out to let me know she needed some assistance in the bathroom—or, as she put it, "I have a *surpriiiise* for you!"—and when I got done with that job (the less said the better, really, although as a longtime volunteer firefighter let me say you just never know when that hazmat training is gonna come in handy) we washed up and headed for the door. As I reached for the switch, Jane jumped in front of me and said, "No, Daddy, I can do it." And without that stick she reached up and up and then got on her tippy-tippy toes and—*click*—off went the light. And *crack* went my heart. Because I was happy for her, sure, and real proud, but I also felt like I had stepped off into a black hole and was trying to grab armfuls of time.

You can't slow it down, though. And you can't wallow in the past. Can't spend your life—as I wrote recently—in a hesternal funk. (*Hesternal* means yesterday, basically.) So the night our new chicken coop was finished, and the floor was still clean, and inside it smelled of fresh wood, Amy and I—Amy, the little girl who is now nearly as tall as me—unrolled our sleeping bags on the floor and camped there overnight. We giggled and spoke in the voices of imaginary chickens. In the dark after Amy was asleep, I smelled cool night air and kiln-dried pine and I listened to her breathe and I ignored the vanishing past and speeding future and instead fell gratefully asleep in the wholehearted present.

TYPHOID MARY

Recently my wife went away from Sunday to Sunday to help one of her sisters with a new baby, so I was nominally in charge, which meant supper sometimes happened in a rush and with ingredients not normally associated with each other, although I will take it as a point of personal pride that we made it clear to Friday before the old man bolted into the supermarket for a frozen pizza. And even then I made it my own by adding barbecue sauce and sliced dill pickles. Why I do not have my own cooking show I do not know.

At one point during our week, Jane, the younger of my daughters, had a bad dream and got a case of the missing-mommy weepies, so I wound up sleeping by her side. In the morning I awoke to see her sweet face three inches from mine, at which point she laid a cough on me like a two-pack-a-day coal miner. I don't know what she caught, but by midmorning we decided only one word really described it, and that word was *phlegm-tastic*.

And now I've got it. I don't get sick often, which is much more a testament to my genetics than to nutrition and lifestyle. But the last two times I've caught something, I've caught it from my blue-eyed younger daughter. Last winter it was strep. She brought it home from preschool. Gave it to her sister. Then her mom. Finally, me. And naturally, by the time I got it, she was all better. So there we were, the grownups, slumping and hacking and lump-throating around trying to get the kids off to bed, and there's the one who started it all, now healthy and happy as you please and hippety-skipping around the house yodeling joy-joy songs at the top of her lungs, and I thought, "Why, you . . . you . . ."

Oh, but you are so happy to see them well again. Iowa singer-songwriter Greg Brown has a song called "Say a Little Prayer," and if you've ever walked the floor with a fevered child in your arms, just yearning for that child to be well again, you will understand that whatever else Greg Brown might have been or be, he knows what it is to be a worried dad in the dark hours.

This latest affliction is blessedly free of fever or anything more serious than a chest-wracking cough and stuffy head and itchy ears, but I will say that at this moment my eyeballs feel as if they have been rolled in sand and someone has overinflated my brain. Naturally, as I cradle my box of Kleenex and wonder when I'll recover the ability to taste anything milder than Triple-X horseradish sauce, the little one who started all this is well on the road to hale and hearty and wondering why Dad is dragging. Last night when I put her to bed we read two books, and then I told her a funny story using my comical stuffy-nose voice, and then I placed my hand on her fever-free brow and leaned down and gave her a kiss and whispered in her ear, "I love you, little Typhoid Mary . . ."

THAT CAT

Back home on the farm I have been contemplating my status in the realm. The trigger for this introspection is a black cat, probably even now this very dang second lying snoozily belly up in the recliner by the window, deep in the dreams of the mice he's not catching, or the frankly fishy treats I'm financing in order to supplement any nutrients he might have missed in the process of being professionally languorous. Cats are the grand mavens of languor. At least when a dog dreams about hunting, its feet twitch. This reflects a certain goofball dedication to the cause, even if it is only in doggie dreamworld. The only cause that cat is dedicated to is: that cat.

That cat first appeared in my life riding a wave of blue-eyed beseechment, which is to say the first time I saw him he was framed in my elder daughter's arms, as she and her sister looked up at me with the sort of sad cotton-candy gaze normally reserved for cheap velvet paintings and suspect charity infomercials.

I held the line for upwards of twenty seconds. Then I said yes, trying my best to sound grumpy. There were ground rules, of course, regarding the feeding and the watering and the outer limits of kitty's health insurance.

Above all—and I believe I even raised one finger and said, "Above all"—I stated in unequivocal terms that we live on a farm, and this would be a barn cat, and barn cats do not live in the house because then we would call them house cats.

• • •

I have to push "pause" here for a moment. I am fully aware that there is nothing more dangerous to one's career than speaking in public on the subject of cats. You can call the president an alien communard, imply that the Statue of Liberty is a man, and recommend that NASCAR go all-electric and race clockwise and you'll collect a few uppity emails and half-star reviews, but say the wrong thing about a cat and you'll find out exactly what it feels like to be chewed up and spit out as a human hairball. So I am proceeding advisedly here. Save your letters; I am a farmboy slow to progress but progressing nonetheless. If you find me a philistine on the feline front, feel free to punish me by sending five swear-dollars to your local humane society, and yes, we neutered.

So the cat became a familiar fixture, rubbing at our ankles on summer evenings when we ate supper on the deck, bringing fresh gophers to the children as they played on the swingset, and infusing the sandbox with a whole new treasure-hunt element. As I am tender of heart, I arranged a large pile of oat straw in one corner of the old granary, where the cat quickly took up residence, his food and water close at hand and the granary mice delivering themselves right to his paws as conveniently as if he had ordered them by phone.

Then it got cold. There were several additional rounds of blue-eyed beseechment. I returned fire with tales of the barn cats of my youth. I spoke of their vigor, I spoke of their thick fur, I spoke of their obvious disdain for the hearth as a place for a cat of any character. On that last point I admit I may have been overspeaking on behalf of the cats. I also omitted the fact that they lived in a barn filled with Holsteins and in fact so loved the warmth of the cows that when a cow stood after lying down, the cats quickly curled up on the toasty spot for a nap. Sadly, when a cow decides to lie back down, she does so with a mighty flop, and it was not unusual to raise a cow for milking only to discover a cat that had been pressed like a daisy in a dictionary. Pancake kitties, we called them.

Oops, there we go, five bucks to the humane association.

Then it got really cold. Okay, fine, I said, but just until it gets back up above zero, and during the day out he goes.

There are times—mostly when I am home alone—that I look in the mirror and assure myself that I am the man of the house. Of course this is true by default, as I am the only male in residence and thus hold the position by chromosome rather than qualification and am perhaps more accurately described as odd man out in the sorority house.

Nonetheless. A guy is a guy. He'll stand there in front of that mirror, right in front of the six square inches of counter space he's allowed, and he'll say, *You sir, you are king of this castle,* and he'll hitch his man-pants and head down the hall, and there he will see a cat, somehow stretched out about three feet long on the rug in front of the woodstove, absorbing heat generated by firewood the man cut, split, stacked, unstacked, hauled to the house, restacked, and got up before dawn to light, and what that man will do is gather up that cat, carry it to the recliner, put it on his lap, and when his wife and daughters return they will find both of the men of the house fast asleep.

USED CAR SHOPPING

We've been shopping for a new car. Well, not a new car, a differ-ent car. We want a different car because the transmission in our current car has reached its teen years, and right on schedule it got all moody, then it began to sulk at stoplights, and now it simply grunts and refuses to engage with the rest of the power train, meaning we basically have four options: raise a canvas sail, tell the kids to get out and push, cut a big hole in the floor and hit the road Fred Flintstone style, or get a different car. Of course we could replace the delinquent transmission, but that would frankly triple the value of the vehicle in question, so now we're back to different.

And of course by different I also mean used, a term that doesn't bother me in the least, especially since the alternative euphemisms—including *previously owned* and *previously driven*—are part of an ongoing stealth campaign to camouflage all of real-ity with two parts spackle and one part sparkle, although neither of that pair comes within a three-thousand-mile oil change of the recently deployed term *reprocessed vehicle,* a real neologismic toe-curler that is the equivalent of sand in in my mental gearbox and sounds as if it was composed by a committee including a cold-hearted prison warden, an expert on industrial food extrusion, and, well, a used car dealer with denial issues.

We don't mind used. It fits our budget and furthermore, based on the way we've treated the one new car we've ever owned, used is exactly what we deserve. You drive off the lot swearing you'll never ever sully the squeaky-clean seat covers and within a week there is loose change in the defroster, snowboot prints on the ceiling, and the heater smells of yogurt splatter.

Also, I keep saying used car, when in truth we're shopping for a used mini-v . . . mini-v . . . y'know, I swore a long time ago you'd never catch me in one of those, so let's just call it the fambulance.

Car shopping is tough for me, because I am just not a car guy. I could give two rips what I'm driving, the sole exception being certain old pickup trucks that are not so much vehicles as loyal companions. Therefore, as with most grownup decisions in our family, my wife is taking the lead, calling dealers, setting up test drives, and consulting a multitude of online car-buying guides. When I started the fire on a recent cool morning, the weekly shopper was laden with circles and underlines and lists of pros and cons. I have done my part by accompanying her on follow-up test drives with salesmen, reconnoitering with Craigslist strangers in Walmart parking lots, kicking tires, looking for oil leaks, and talking the kids down when they realize there's a pretty good shot that not only will our vehicle not include a DVD player, it may have rolled off the line before DVDs were even invented. Shoot, the first used fambulance we bought had been rewired so you had to run the wipers using a standard electrical wall switch.

Nearly a month has passed since we started looking. My wife and I are great at talking everything through and weighing all our options. We are not so great at pulling the trigger. We've had to borrow a car from a friend to get us through this patch. He has no children, so after he gets the car back he'll probably roll a few miles before he stops wondering where we put the off-brand air freshener and realizes that's just what raspberry yogurt smells like after two weeks in the heater.

FIREWOOD FRIEND

I got a bunch of wood split the other day, which is good because we were down to nothin' but bark last "spring" when we got one final blast of the white stuff and I had to beg some wood off my buddy Mills. I didn't actually have to beg, I just mentioned to him that we were caught short, and the next time I came home there was a quarter cord stacked right there in the garage. That's the kind of friend Mills is.

Mills and I met about twenty-five years ago back when we were both green EMTs. My first recollection is of him and me down in a ditch in the dark, struggling to extricate some drunk guy wearing a split lip and a bloody yellow tie. Sometime after that we were standing around an ambulance bay at 3 a.m. and he got to talking about how he'd been bowfishing—or, to put it less artfully, shooting carp with a bow and arrow. To a knuckle-head of my extraction, the idea of combining archery and fishing seemed about as good as it gets, so I convinced Mills to take me, and before long we were sneaking off to shoot carp the way some guys sneak off to shoot pool. Mills even took me to his favorite spot, a fallen tree he called the Widowmaker that lay parallel to a channel filled with foraging carp.

You don't take someone to your favorite carp-shooting spot unless you're ready to make a long-term commitment. Soon Mills and I were doing all the things real friends do. I helped him move, then he helped me move. I smashed my knuckles helping him put a refrigerator down the right-angle stairs to his basement; he smashed his helping me wrassle a vintage stove the size of a Hereford through two porch doors and into my kitchen. We enabled each other's hoarding tendencies by trading eBay links, buying things out from underneath each other on Craigslist, and dumpster diving together for the bricks left over from the construction of a convenience store because you never know when yer gonna need bricks. We walked each other through long-slog-stretches when one of our hearts was busted and shared in the happiness when we found the light again.

When Mills needed a eulogy for a man he admired, he asked for my help and I gave it; when my wife decided to have our daughter at home, I called Mills because I knew he had delivered six babies in emergency situations. He waited in the garage until our baby was safely arrived. After offering congratulations, he said, "Need anything?" and I said, "Nope," and off he went, and now I say that among the bedrock gifts of time are friendships expressible in five syllables or less.

I don't care for the term *best friend*. It's too brittle. Friendships shift and adjust along with the rest of your life. I think of my friend Frank, who knows my every dark secret and who introduced me to the poetry that changed my life; or my friend Gene, who bore to me the ring with which I married my wife. Or my wife, who is every bit the friend these men are to me and so much more.

Rivers rise and fall, and one day we went to the Widowmaker and it wasn't there, having been swept away by a spring flood. We never really found a spot that good again. And truth be told, Mills and I don't do much carp shooting anymore. But a quarter-century gone, we're still making ambulance calls together. These days he's a veteran professional paramedic and I'm a veteran volunteer first responder. When people need help, they call us. And when I need help—or a quarter cord of split oak—I call Mills.

TOUGH GRANNY

Guests for this Big Top show included the group Different Drums of Ireland. My Grandma Perry cherished her Irish heritage, so it seemed natural to build the monologue around her memory.

My Grandma Perry was quite a grandma. Not exactly the bake-you-a-batch-of-brownies type of grandma, that's for sure. More like a heat-up-the-store-bought-pineapple-ham-loaf-while-I-work-my-way-through-a-second-pack-of-Carlton-100s grandma. I can still see her doing the ironing, one of those sandbag ashtrays at the pointy end of the ironing board, that Carlton dangling from her lips, and every one of Grandpa's shirts pressed straight and sharp, with here and there an ashy little skid mark. She chewed Clark's Teaberry gum, wadding it up and sticking it to the cellophane of her cigarette pack when it was time to light up. And every one of her grandkids—me included—remembers the day we told Grandma smoking was bad for her health, at which point we found out that telling Grandma smoking was bad for her health was bad for our health. Sawed off and short tempered, she was fond of saying things like "well, hell-up-a-tree" and "that cheapskate is tighter than a gnat's hinder around a rain barrel." To say Grandma was outspoken was to say that whenever someone asked me if I was related to Wanda Perry I always said, "Well, who's asking, and why?"

She loved to drink iced tea and play Yahtzee even when we were so young we messed up the scorecards. She was always ready to go fishing in her lucky fishing cap, and when she reeled in those sunfish she held the handle of her fishing reel between her thumb and third finger so as to free up the index and middle finger for the ever-present heater. She'd pack us into her Plymouth Duster and take us to walk dogs at the humane association—a humane association she herself helped found, because for all her roughness, Grandma's credo and favorite phrase was that we should be a voice for those who cannot speak. She backed it up with her care for thousands of strays over the years, more than a few humans included. She knew her way to the bail window of the county jail, and I was present more than once when someone showed up with a wrinkled check to make good on their bail money.

And when one of her roughneck grandsons showed an interest in poetry, Grandma not only encouraged him, she collected everything he wrote, even framing a few chosen poems and keeping them on the wall years beyond the time he realized they weren't very good—by which time her encouragement had seen him well down the road to a life of putting words in a line in one fashion or another.

Grandma was well into her eighties before time caught up with her. She had a few years in the nursing home, where she used to get me to sneak her cigarettes against the rules, and if you have a problem with that, well, you talk to Grandma. Right before she died—quite literally hours—I had the chance to thank her for hanging up those poems and encouraging the knuckle-headed boy who wrote them, because she changed his life, and he is forever grateful.

Grandma's been gone a handful of years now. At her funeral we sang "My Wild Irish Rose" as she had requested we do since way back when we were tots. It was a sweet promise to keep. And so now as we return to the Big Top stage and as Different Drums of Ireland is joined by the Ojibwe Singers, I will close my eyes, let myself float off to the land of my grandmother's ancestors, and—you and the surgeon general will just have to bear with me, here—fire up an imaginary Carlton 100.

THE WHITE PINE

We've got a gigantic old pine tree in the front yard. Takes an adult and two tots to reach around it. Some of the limbs alone are so thick you could saw 'em off, stand 'em on end, and they'd make a tree in their own right. Aesthetically speaking, the tree is a tad on the gnarly side, as over the years some of those larger limbs have succumbed to wet snow, high winds, and gentle hints from the house insurance underwriter. The trunk is festered up with a lot of sappy nubs and gaps where the severed limbs used to be.

Way up high you can see an old chunk of rope some kid slung over a limb decades ago. I say decades ago because the limb has swallowed the rope and only a frayed stub of it is visible, the rest enclosed in bark. The rope seems way too high up to have been used for a swing, so I imagine the kid up there fixing some sort of secret hideout pulley system, his or her pants and palms all sticky with pitch, the summer breeze soft in the green needles, the long-ago country day unfolding lazily and expansively, the way childhood days do. 'Course, too, it could have been some farmer rigging an engine hoist when the tree was younger and the limb was closer to earth. Or maybe someone hung a buck deer there once and skinned it under the yard light in the cold and just never undid the rope.

Shortly after we moved here my elder daughter asked for a tire swing, so on a Sunday afternoon my brother and I selected a limb from the big pine and hung one. It's your classic: a chunk of old rope cinched around an old wore-out truck tire. There's a scuffed patch in the grass directly beneath it now from all the feet come to climb aboard, and it's a rare visiting youngster who doesn't bail from the mini-van and sprint headlong for that old tire beneath that old tree. Sometimes two or three kids pile on, and yet the limb above barely flexes, anchored as it is to a trunk as solid as a silo. Five years gone already and the girl who first requested that swing is now a teenager, but I still see her out there now and then, swaying back and forth on the four-ply snow-tire pendulum beneath the canopy of all those green needles. It warms my heart to think the chance to swing in the shade of that pine tree still—now and then—trumps texting, makeup, and earbuds.

The day is not far off when we'll have to take that tree down. The last limb it lost hit our house. It took a divot from the shingles and left a rumple in the rain gutters. It struck the roof with a mighty whack and the ground with a mighty thud. We all ran out to see what had happened, which upon reflection is not really the way to behave when giant branches are falling from the sky, but human nature is an inquisitive little gerbil.

The thing is, that pine tree stands right outside my bedroom window. Thoughtful ponderments and reminiscence aside, if we let it become too weakened, some stormy night it could whomp me in my sleep. Still, I'm dragging my feet. We'll hate to see that tree go, even as the more practical me notes that there are thousands of trees within sight of that one, and perhaps out there is some sad little sapling that needs love too. As a backup we have hung a second tire swing in a big old sugar maple across the yard.

Even if that pine goes down tomorrow, my children will remember what it was to take its shade. What it was to look up from the road across the valley and identify our place by that white pine's misshapen silhouette. The morning after the most recent limb came crashing to earth, I fetched the chainsaw and blocked it up. After it was split and dried we burned it in the woodstove. Like all pine it went to flame fast and hot, but even the short-lived heat was more than the old tree owed us.

CHRISTMAS TREE KIDS

Whatever the month, we already have our Christmas tree. It's back behind the pole barn. That's where they all are.

I was never a Christmas tree guy. In part this was due to the counterintuitive fact that I was raised in an obscure Christian church so fundamental the December holiday was viewed as dangerously contrived pagan silliness. So when I was growing up we never had a Christmas tree in the house. We did get Christmas, because my grandma was a believer of a different stripe. She always bought a squat Scotch pine, and some years the pile of presents dwarfed the tree.

Later I left the church and was freed up to get a tree, but by then I was a bachelor and never had reason or interest in dressing or decorating my digs holiday-wise. Y'know, you got some deer horns and a concert poster on the wall, why mess with the vibe? Plus based on my housekeeping history, last year's Christmas tree skeleton would still be standing.

Also, once after Grandpa died I helped Grandma put up her annual Scotch pine, and the whole deal kinda cured me of Christmas trees in general. She had one of those plastic stands with the three screws, and every time I got the tree halfway vertical and tightened one of the screws, the tree would tip over. And just the same as smoke from a campfire always seems to swing around and blow your way, no matter which screw I was tightening, no matter from what angle, that tree always seemed to manage to fall my way. The needles on a Scotch pine take the term *needles* very seriously, and by the time I got that blankety-blank tree to stand upright I felt like I'd been loofahed with an overactive porcupine.

Oh, and the language: profoundly un-Christmassy.

Anyways, for years I didn't have a Christmas tree. Then I got married and my wife brought with her a beautiful young girl named Amy, who's now my daughter. To my eternal shame, when our first Christmas rolled around I still held out. We did decorate the house, but I didn't think we needed a tree. Plus, we were going to visit Grandma. But then we moved to a farm and there were Christmas trees growing right out back. So the second week of December we went ahead and cut one. I was reluctant, but Amy's eyes lit right up. She helped me saw it down, drag it in, and put it up. And now come the day after Thanksgiving I'm the first one lobbying to grab the saw and get out there.

We cut last year's tree out on the ridge, Amy taking her turn on the bucksaw while Jane, our youngest, played in the snow with our black cat. We hauled the tree and the little one back home in a sled. Halfway down the trail I took a picture of Anneliese and the girls and the tree. In the photo all three of them are looking at me with blue eyes and smiles, the tree settled on the sled between them.

We brought the tree inside and spent the evening stringing popcorn beside the fire and letting the girls take turns hanging ornaments. Later, when Anneliese was putting Jane to bed, I was in the kitchen doing dishes when I noticed the living room lights go out. I looked, and there was Amy sitting sideways in the old overstuffed chair, legs dangling, staring at the lit tree in the dark. You want, in moments like these, to just shut the world down and call it a day. And when I pulled that dishwater drain, that's exactly what I did: went in and sat with her.

That tree was a spruce, short and a tad gappy, although nowhere near Charlie Brown status. But it looked perfectly beautiful glowing in the corner that evening. I got to thinking about how long I'd held out against getting a Christmas tree, and how the kids coming along changed things, and what lesson I might take from that. And I believe those first Christmas trees taught me that sometimes you need to stop being the man you think you are, and start being the man you oughta be.

Merry Christmas.

NEVERENDING NEW YEAR

The older I grow, the less I'm interested in celebrating Official New Year's. Oh, I don't mind a get-together if it's with good friends and convenient, but by and large I prefer celebrating any given Tuesday.

For a few years in my early teens we spent New Year's Eve at Grandma Perry's house. Grandma was overgenerous, and by the time New Year's rolled around, we kids were saturated with store-bought gifts, store-bought peanut brittle, store-bought angel food candy, and store-bought stuff in general. Being raised on home-made and hand-me-downs, my brothers and sisters and I had an uncritical appetite for all things store-bought and didn't feel slighted in the least that our grandma was not a homebaked-sugar-cookies kind of grandma. Besides, when she did do her once-a-year Christmas baking—mainly those red and green spritz cookies manufactured by a process of cold extrusion using a device similar to a caulking gun—they always tasted of Carlton 100 smoke, which had of course been kneaded into the dough with love. With Grandma you didn't just breathe her secondhand smoke, you ate it too.

So New Year's Eve would arrive, and by a quarter of midnight the rest of the family would be gone abed and it was just me in Grandma's living room, and I'd be coming down off a sustained sugar high, modulating ever so preciously into the spun sugar haze of teen angst as I sat there in my feathered hair and new velour shirt gazing out Grandma's picture window at the red light of a radio tower blinking softly atop a hill just up the road.

Grandma had a bookshelf clock that chimed on the hour and half-hour, and it seemed to me the tick-tock of that clock was carefully timed to the backbeat of the pulsing red light on the hill, and as the seconds ticked their way toward midnight I found my entire being suffused with an impossible nostalgia as—at fourteen, or whatever—I sensed the implacable passage of time and the looming finality of life, or at least this year's peanut brittle.

When the clock rang midnight, I felt as if I were floating out above the reverberant chasm of an unknown future.

As you can see, I was a very poetic sort of youth. On the inside, anyway.

Probably my favorite New Year's ever was the one I spent with the New Auburn Area Fire Department on the evening of December 31, 1999—eve of the much dreaded Y2K. We were all ready down there at the hall, although we weren't clear on how we might prevent the collapse of civilized society with two pike poles, five yellow fire trucks, and several sheets of Stop, Drop, and Roll stickers. In the end we just watched *Tommy Boy* and ate a tankerload of Lil' Smokies. By half past midnight the lights were still on and no one had come to take away our deer rifles, so we unplugged the Crock Pots and went home.

But these days I take a New Year whenever I can get it. Sometimes you need a New Year when you see the electric bill. Sometimes you need a New Year when the health insurance premium comes due, or when your pet goat dies, or when the hail defenestrates your greenhouse. Sometimes you need the one you love to grant you a New Year after you inadvertently mow off her flower garden.

And New Year's resolutions? I make them every night. I resolve to be more patient, I resolve to be more frugal, I resolve not to gorge myself on jalapeño cheddar corn curlies right before bedtime. I resolve to resolve to demonstrate greater resolve.

These resolutions rarely take. But hallelujah, because you know what? Tomorrow is New Year's Day. Again.

A SENSE OF PITCH

Johnny Cash, Joan Baez, Merle Haggard, Willie Nelson, the Indigo Girls, Brandi Carlile, Bill Monroe, Rickie Lee Jones, John Hiatt, Trampled by Turtles, Joan Osborne, Lyle Lovett, Emmylou Harris, the Nitty Gritty Dirt Band, Bela Fleck, Nickel Creek . . . Right down to its own Blue Canvas Orchestra and singers, the Lake Superior Big Top Chautauqua tent has gift-wrapped and presented hundreds of musical acts to its visitors over the years. It's only natural, then, that the scent of canvas often leads me to consider the power of music and those who make it.

HAPPY MOURNING MUSIC

Some of the music played in the Big Top Chautauqua tent is new, some is vintage. I wrote this monologue for a show featuring the Temptations.

Welcome back to *Tent Show Radio,* folks, from the backstage dressing room with the one lonely little lightbulb burnin' . . .

I'm back here reflecting on the hits of the Temptations and how music has the power to evoke long-gone days. A few weeks back the tent hosted the group Great Big Sea, and when they did a cover of Slade's "Run, Runaway," it caught me completely off guard and whipped me back in a trice to a weed patch behind a machine shop on a ranch in Wyoming, where the air smelled of sage and turpentine and I was listening to the song on a Walkman while I stripped poles for a corral. Even more than the power of evocation, however, I'm fascinated by how we *use* that power. Back in my feckless bachelor days, there was this pop song called "Drops of Jupiter." It was a beautifully overproduced musical tidbit. In my teens I would have wallowed in it. In my late twenties I would have sneered at it. In my mid-thirties—having been told by a friend that there are no guilty pleasures, only pleasures—I simply enjoyed it. The first time I heard it I grinned and turned it up. There were strings and longing and a sweeping chorus, and just as I thought, *The only thing missing here is some na-nas,* the *na-nas* kicked in.

Right about the time this song hit, I got a new girlfriend. Wherever I was when I heard the song, I'd think of her. Then, when things eventually went unignorably south, I really couldn't bear to hear "Drops of Jupiter" anymore. I'd punch the radio button desperately hoping for some George Jones. There was a stretch of the usual pale-hearted navel-gazing. But then one day a year or so on down the line, I was running errands and "Drops of Jupiter" came on the radio, and I liked it again. I listened to the whole thing straight through with nary a liver-twinge, and when it ended I remember thinking, *Put me in again, coach.*

Shortly after my second daughter was born, I lost my dear friend Tim. We were the same age, and the news was a shock. When we first met I used to listen to his vinyl Pink Floyd collection while I wrote, and over the years he had taken me to live shows in England that completely redirected my musical life. I in turn introduced him to Marty Stuart, Steve Earle, Dwight Yoakam, and Waylon Jennings. You really haven't lived until you've seen a pint-sized drunken Englishman whoopin' it up at a Confederate Railroad show.

Tim—I called him Swifty—was from the Midlands of England, an ocean away, and there would be no funeral. A day after I got the news I went down to the pole barn and started digging through boxes of old CDs, pulling everything that reminded me of the music Swifty and I listened to on our English rambles: the Waterboys, Marillion, Simple Minds, Siouxsie and the Banshees, the Cure, Bronski Beat, Roxy Music, Status Quo . . . Back in my writing room I played them over and over, every song cutting loose new-old memories, and sure, some tears.

It's a fine line that separates wallowing from remembrance, but as I listened to those songs late into the night, I didn't care. Track by track I was back with Tim, riding shotgun in the left-hand passenger seat of his Mini, strap-hanging on the Tube in London, or simply shuffling home from the local pub. By the time the sun came up I had sorted some things out and stored some things away. And now when I'm running down some Wisconsin backroad with Status Quo in the deck and the three-chord stomp of "Rollin' Home" comes thumping from the speakers, I grin and cast my eyes to the right, where I can see Swifty, with his hand-rolled cigarette and easy grin, and I'm thankful right down to my boots for the time-bending power of music.

COOLSVILLE

Rickie Lee Jones was the guest for this show. She is cool in the coolest sense. That got me to thinking about what it is to be cool.

Welcome back to *Tent Show Radio,* folks, from the backstage dressing room with the one lonely little lightbulb burnin' . . .

Y'know, I'm just sittin' here listening to Rickie Lee Jones and considering the idea of what it is to be cool. What it is, and how to have it. How to get it. Cool is ineffable. Cool is about presence as much as action. You can't force it, you can't fake it, you can't chase after it. Because, well, that wouldn't be cool. Maybe you can earn cool, I'm not sure. I know you can own it.

Willie Nelson is cool. Willie Nelson is cool because he can wear braids and running shoes and play golf and still be cool and that is a powerful cool indeed. I bring up Willie a lot when I get in discussions about cool and the difficulty of remaining cool. For instance, for a moment back in the 1980s David Lee Roth was cool. No, seriously—put aside your bald jokes and your perpetual failed reunion tours—but at some point the spandex tights have got to go. Whereas Willie's deal is still cool because he makes it seem as if he's just ramblin' along, and you can ramble when you're sixty or seventy or more whereas the scissor-kicks are harder to come by.

Aretha Franklin is cool. Nina Simone was cool. Julia Child was cool. Joan Jett was and is cool. Sade is cooler than cool. Emergency room nurses are by and large cool. Cool transcends occupation, although tonight I'm leaning heavily on music.

Ray Charles was cool. There's a shot that Ray Charles was the coolest of the cool. For all time, really. Ray was cool right into the grave. (Although perhaps if you talked with a Raylette or two you'd discover that even the coolest cool is a matter of perspective, or distance. Cool should not be confused with good behavior.) There's a moment in Ray's version of "Do I Ever Cross Your Mind" when he sings the words *melancholy jailer* and his delivery of the word *jail-ah* has enough cool in it to last me three years if only I could pull it off. And that's the other intangible element of coolness. Part of being cool is knowing when you're not cool and just letting it ride. You know—it's okay to sing along with Ray when you're alone, but shame on you if you think you're gettin' anywhere close to Ray. There's this moment on a Ray album I own when he's singing "America the Beautiful" and he breaks it down a little, prefaces the chorus by saying, "*And you know when I was in school we used to sing it something like this here . . .*," and every time I hear that part, all I can think is, *Oh, Ray—you went to a different school than I.*

Cool doesn't admit confusion. Cool brooks no uncertainty. So, I mean, that's me out. I'm a bundle of self-doubt and contradiction. That doesn't mean I'm unhappy or ungrateful, I'm just not cool.

I do think you can be temporarily cool. I've been cool a couple of times. It usually doesn't last more than ten seconds, usually until I shut my seatbelt in the door or realize I have my T-shirt on backwards. The second I start feeling cool, I check my fly.

My all-time record for being cool is about three minutes. I was backstage at this deal and a very famous lady walked up and stood beside me. We were a good distance from the stage, and it was quiet enough to have a conversation, but I could still hear the sound of thirty-five thousand people out there screaming to see her. She seemed to be enjoying her teensy little pond of solitude, and in the moment I figured the coolest thing I could do was let her have an interlude of nobody tugging or talking at her. We just stood silently shoulder to shoulder, two people watching the show prep go on around us, right up until the second she was whisked off to resume being capital V, capital F, Very Famous.

Well, of course I'm not gonna tell you who it was.

Wouldn't be cool.

STEVE EARLE, LIFE COACH

*The history of Steve Earle begins back in Texas when, as
a teenager, he hit the road in search of a musical life and
found it. Under the tutelage of folks like Townes Van Zandt
and Guy Clark, the young Steve Earle established himself as
a songwriter who blended poetry, story, and grit in a way
that made his work instantly recognizable, whether sung
by him or stars like Willie Nelson and Emmylou Harris. For
a while there he was country music's headlining big deal,
and then the road forked like the devil's tongue and there
were some years spent more in the ditch than on the road,
but the man came roaring back, and whatever the state of
his situation, the state of his art has never wavered: unapol-
ogetic, uncompromising, and managing to contain both the*
diamond *and* the rough.

*Now and then he plays in the big blue tent. This is from
one of those nights.*

Welcome back to *Tent Show Radio,* folks, from the backstage
dressing room with the one lonely little lightbulb burnin' . . .

Back home on the farm somewhere down in the pole barn
there is a box and in that box is a nonfunctioning cassette tape
with the name of the album displayed across the j-card in the
form of a big green-and-white highway sign. For years I thought
the sign said Exit Oh, but then one day I heard the man who made
the album say it "Exit Zero," and I thought well, of course, and

added this incident to the infinite list of times I've been a little slow on the ol' uptake.

I got started on Steve Earle thanks to *Guitar Town,* and even tonight I was eager to hear the staccato poetry of the title song— *I got a two-pack habit and a motel tan*—but it was *Exit 0* that really set my feet to itching in every sense. I remember standing on the deck of a John Deere B, raking hay on my dad's farm with the throttle wide open and *Exit 0* on the Walkman headphones, my heart impatient, the highway on my mind.

In short order I became a hardcore Steve Earle fan and proselyte, able to recite his albums in order and name his touring band and all of his five or six ex-wives, and I once found myself so moved by one of his performances in Birmingham, England, that I became *that* guy and hollered, "All the way from Wisconsin!" and "*WOOO!!!*" while he was tuning. "Man," said Mister Earle, "yer lost."

I've never—even at the peak of fandom—been a hero worshipper. I remember my dad getting grumpy with me when, like so many of my age, I discovered the Beatles only after John Lennon got shot. I went around plaintively crooning, "All we are saying . . ." but even then the farm-booted church-boy part of me had a firm grip on the idea that life requires more heavy lifting than a pop song can provide. And so it was with Steve Earle. I knew I had to do my own work, I knew it wouldn't likely change the world, but it was his songs that built a fire in my belly. Or at least beneath my butt.

◆ ◆ ◆

In 1991 Steve Earle recorded a live album called *Shut Up and Die Like an Aviator.* He was on a grungy downhill slide and sang like a man forcing up crushed glass. Right near the beginning of track 10 some audience member hollered something and Steve responded with a simple, declarative "Doin' fine."

He wasn't, of course. As a matter of fact, right around the time I was listening to that album he was likely in jail, or under a bridge, or in a pawn shop in East Nashville. But he survived all that and came back.

The albums have stacked up now, the cassettes became CDs, the CDs became digits, and I've been grateful for every bit of it, even the stuff I didn't quite get. But for me it will always come back to *Exit 0,* because what I heard above the pop-pop of that John Deere was music that suggested folks from small towns and unpolished circumstances might try their hand at art as well, and that there was a life somewhere between low-down and uptown, and although I'm never quite where I want to be and certainly never where I ought to be, I am where I am because Steve Earle put up that big green exit sign.

I don't feel the need to scream "*Wooo!*" tonight. I'm just content to kick back and listen to good work by a guy still standing in his own boots. Steve Earle. All these years. And y'know what?

He's doin' fine.

ADVICE FROM A GRAMMY WINNER

*I wrote this monologue for a Big Top show that featured me
with my band, the Long Beds.*

Sometimes I drag out a guitar and work on a song. Things never
get too complicated. Oh, every once in a while I toss in a busted
fourth or a jazzy clam just to keep it real, but things never stray
far from 4/4. I call it the clodhopper beat.

I grew up singing in church. Again, it was nothing fancy. No
choir, no robes, you just sat in your chair and tried to find the
notes. Sometimes my brother and I worked out simple harmonies,
and once in a blue moon someone might play piano, but it was all
basics, no boogie-woogie, lest the devil get your toe tapping off
toward the path of wickedness.

Mom had a record player—a phonograph—in the house, and
one of those big boxy Reader's Digest music collections, each
vinyl disk tucked in its own sleeve, and there was a song on there
us kids just loved called "A Boy Named Sue," sung by Johnny
Cash. We learned all the words to that one, and it's a wonder we
didn't scratch it right off, we picked the needle up at the end and
dropped it back at the beginning so many times.

After Johnny Cash I skippity-doodled around listening to pop
music for a while, then one day in Wyoming my boss and I were
bombin' along in a four-wheel-drive ranch truck when we hit
a hidden irrigation ditch and went airborne. When we landed,
everything inside that truck was jarred loose and out from be-

neath the seat flew an eight-track tape. I picked it up, looked at it, looked at my boss, then asked, "Who's Waylon Jennings?"

"Son," he said, pointing at the eight-track player in the dash, "you need to jam that thing in there." And of course I heard the boogety-boogety and the whoop-whoop-whoop and was hooked forevermore.

I'll stop right there, because if you start listing influences it can sound as if you're claiming some sort of equivalency, and I'm under no such illusion. I'm a typist who is now and then allowed to hang his words on a D chord and perform them aloud. I stand onstage with my poor patient guitar like some musical Walter Mitty, surrounded by true musicians who bear me carefully along while I just stand there and sing from my boots. My band is called the Long Beds but I've often said they should be called the Bowling Bumpers, because the song is a bowling lane, and I am a lumpy bowling ball, and I start rolling along and kinda veer off to one side or reverse verses or maybe get to thinking about whether or not I remembered to jiggle the handle on the toilet before I left home, and gently as you please the band nudges me back into the lane and keeps me rolling along until finally I get to the end of the song and knock down a few pins and then they smile at me like it's the best anyone could hope for.

Early on I'd get real nervous before we played. Then finally one show came along when we walked out before a decent-sized audience and I found myself more eager to play than nervous to play. I strapped on that ol' Larrivée acoustic with the International Harvester decal on it, began boldly strumming a hefty open E, and strode toward the mic. At the last minute I turned back to survey the band. I wanted to make sure everyone was set to go, but I also wanted to make sure they saw in the eyes of their leader that there was nothing to fear. I noticed one of the fellows, a young man who would go on to Grammy-winning fame, jerking his head at me in a "c'mere" sorta way. And so, still strumming—I was feeling professional, after all—I walked back and leaned in and put my ear down where I could hear him, and he said, "Hey—plug in your guitar."

GUITAR GIRLS

I had my guitar out the other day and was noodling around on it, playing a very complicated riff constituted around plucking a D chord over and over and not much else, when Jane, my youngest, climbed up on my lap and started singing made-up lyrics along with my stumblebum strumming. The first verse had something about a dog and a princess, so you know there was some potential there. I threw her a G chord then, and she went with it, which seems like a good sign, like she's got a sense of pitch. Life goes better if you have a sense of pitch. You know, so you can sing along, but also a sense of pitch so you can get a read on folks, maybe figure out if you want to sit in with 'em, kinda try and match their groove—or maybe you wanna move along and hum a different tune.

When her sister, Amy, was the same age, we used to do this very same thing—I'd just strum at nothing in particular, and she'd sing. One day we were noodling along when she stopped, turned her face up to mine, and said, "I want to sing and play with you for all my life." I suppose she wondered why all of a sudden Dad's eyes got all shiny.

There are a lot of reasons why you might wanna learn to play a guitar. I've heard many guys—famous and not famous—say their main reason for learning was so they could get girls. I know Townes Van Zandt said he got his first guitar because he decided it was the shortest route to get girls and Cadillacs just like Elvis got. Of course you don't need a Y chromosome to play six strings.

I'd like it if my girls learned to play guitar sometime, because one thing I've noticed about women who play guitar is that they don't tend to suffer fools. And if they do suffer a fool, why, they put him in a song and run him out of town forever.

I'm afraid my girls won't learn much about playing guitar from their old man. I didn't learn my first guitar chord until I was in my thirties, and when it comes to workin' the ol' fretboard I'm about as clunky as they come—I often say I play guitar with all the nuance of a guy cuttin' brush. But there we were, my younger daughter and I, just easin' along, me going D-A-G, and her going along verse by made-up verse, when—just like her sister all those years before her—she stopped and looked up at me and said, "Daddy, when I sing, my heart feels colorful."

Of course I went all shiny-eyed again.

Nobody's ever gonna plunk down their cash to hear me play guitar solos. Nobody's ever gonna give me a Cadillac for my finger-picking. But twice in my life now I've played just well enough that my daughters said something so pure-hearted that it makes my eyes shine up even this very moment. To all you fellas out there playin' your guitars so you can get girls, eat my dust—I've got two of 'em now. And someday they will be together recalling their childhood days, and one of them will say, "You remember how every time Dad played guitar he'd get all teary? I know he wasn't all that good, but jeepers . . ."

BLUES FOR AMATEURS

The other day I was feeding the chickens and thinking about the blues. Chickens never seem to get the blues. They get the flapping cackles, and the goggle-eyed blinkies, and now and then they get the worm, but you can't really say they get the blues. But you and I, we can get the blues. It should follow, then, that if we are capable of gettin' the blues, of feelin' the blues, we ought to be able to *sing* the blues.

But most of us (I am raising my own hand here) are not. Not only are not, but should not. We've all had our moments alone at the stoplight with Ray Charles, where Ray is singing every single sad note of intangible, inexpressible longing we've ever felt, and he's nailing it, every teensy blue note twist and gutbucket moan so dead-on it's like they were cut from your own heart, and you think, *Yes, Ray, yes, that's it, that's exactly how I feel, and here, let me help you with that a little bit, lemme take a verse . . .* and what follows may feel good but it is the musical equivalent of strangling a chicken.

I heard Ray Wylie Hubbard talking about the late Lightnin' Hopkins the other day, and how Lightnin' played the twelve-bar blues . . . and the thirteen-bar blues . . . and the thirteen-and-a-half-bar blues, Ray Wylie's point being, Lightnin' went to that next chord when Lightnin' was good and ready, and right there is why with just one single *uh-huh* Lightnin' Hopkins can put me on my knees. It's why Hound Dog Taylor can make me feel like a hound dog. It's why he can sing "my baby's gone" and I know he's really talkin' about *my* baby. It's why when he runs that slide up and down the fretboard he might as well be running it up and down my spine. It's why Koko Taylor can make me—a stoic post-Calvinist stiff-upper-lip Scandihoovian paint-by-the-numbers three-chord roots-rock mumbler—squeeze my eyes shut, throw my hands to the sky, do a little altar dance, and say, *Yes, Sister Koko! PREACH, Sister Koko!*

And right there is the most glorious mystery of the blues: how deeply we can feel them as opposed to how poorly we can express them. Sometimes we don't even know that stuff is in us until it comes out of someone else's mouth. You've forgot about how wrong you was done until a man like Charlie Parr or W.C. Clark bends just one note and bends it just so and suddenly you are all amen and hallelujah. You're feeling those blues to your bones. And yet, if you say, *Here, W.C., gimme that microphone, lemme back you up on that,* well, everybody involved is in for a big disappointment.

It's a sad truth: for most of us mere mortals, there's really only one blues song we're qualified to sing, and I'm already working on it. It's a twelve-bar number, maybe twelve and a half, a little thing I like to call "I Got the I Can't Sing the Blues Blues." So far I've got half a verse and the chorus. I figured I'd test it out the other morning when I was feeding the chickens. "Listen here, you birds," I said, "lemme sing you the blues," and then I laid it on 'em blue as I could blow it. When it was over, half of 'em got the flappin' cackles and the other half just stood there giving me the ol' goggle-eyed blinkies. As pretty much any audience would.

LOCK UP THE CHICKENS

"Well, that's farmin'," my farmer father would say whenever things went wrong. In fact, in our family all of us—even the nonfarmers—still use that phrase in the context of bad news. But sometimes when the corn sprouts on time or the chickens really fill the egg basket or I catch my daughter slopping hogs while wearing a ballerina outfit, I say, "Well, that's farmin'."

And I say it with a smile.

ASPARAGUS

Back home on the farm the last of the asparagus has been picked and the remainders are going all frazzled. Lilacs come and go pretty fast, but once the asparagus calls it a day you know summer is running full bore and spring is filed solidly under "Memories."

I cherish that asparagus patch—for the asparagus, sure, because I like asparagus. If you'd have told me when I was fourteen that I would like asparagus, I'd have said you needed to get your brain recalibrated. I used to view it with suspicion when it appeared each spring between the two silos out behind the barn, and with low-level dismay when it appeared in a bowl on the kitchen table. But now I can't wait for that first shoot to break through. I like to study the emergent green fuse knowing in a matter of twenty-four to forty-eight hours it will be pickable and edible, a sign that the subterranean frost has given up its grip. And the greenness of an asparagus spear when steamed! It is a flat-out rebuke to winter, even if the poor little guy was poking up through snow.

So yah, I like asparagus. But I like that asparagus patch even more, because it is one of multitudinous reasons I love my wife. When we moved to the farm Anneliese said she wanted to get an asparagus patch going right away, because it takes three years before the asparagus really comes on. I was busy running off to do one thing or another and didn't really get after it. Part of the problem is that I am the king of instant gratification and just couldn't imagine planting something today so we could enjoy it three years down the road. You will understand now why I am not in the orchard or wine business, and possibly also why my retirement fund could use some attention.

Sometime after she asked, I did see some six-by-sixes (the kind used in landscaping) advertised on Craigslist not so far away, and I headed over to pick them up. My idea was they'd make a good raised bed for the asparagus over along the side of the old granary. But then I had to hit the road again, so a buddy of mine framed them up and put in the raised bed, and my wife started the asparagus while I was gone.

And then *whammo* three years were gone, and then six, and each spring through the rebirthing earth the asparagus comes up plump as Jolly Green Giant fingers. We steam it, we sauté it, we pickle it, we make it into soup, and we even had to wait for our premiere batch this year because the six-year-old got there first and ate the very first arrivals raw, right there in the patch. I caught her at it and didn't say a word. Why would I? She was eating chlorophyll beneath the open sky, a sure-fire long-term antidote to all things electronic and stuffy. On the other hand, when my wife caught the chickens in there the other day, they were lucky to escape with their giblets.

It's miraculous stuff, asparagus. Most miraculous is the apparently impossible rate at which it grows. Take a nap, turn your back, and you've got another batch. And I suppose we appreciate it even more for its cyclic spirit, expressed through brief presence and extended absence. By the time it comes back, we're hungry for it with more than our stomachs.

This year the steamer basket was full from late April through late June, and every single time I snapped off a fistful of spears on my way back from the morning chicken coop chores I considered my wife and how sometimes the best thing she does for me is press ahead on her own so that later I may have the joy of catching up and rejoining her.

UNFARMER

Because I have written about pigs and posed for pictures while holding chickens, I am often introduced as a farmer. Out of respect to the farmers who raised me and those still struggling to pay the banker, let me say that calling me a farmer is like calling a guy who hits himself in the head with a hammer a brain surgeon. We do have a bunch of chickens, and I have been in the hog business for a few years now. First year I had two pigs. Second year I doubled the size of the operation. Got four. Economy of scale, that's where yer profit lies.

I shall never forget the day I got my first pair of feeder pigs. While the farmer and I were lifting the first one into the pickup, I detected a profound pain in my left rear buttock. Upon closer examination I discovered that the farmer's gigantic coon dog—no doubt assuming I was stealing the pigs—had gone stark raving bonkers and was actively masticating a Double-Whopper's worth of my backside.

I'll say this for that dog: he was profoundly dedicated to his task. By the time he turned me loose I felt like my backside had been run through a laundry mangler. Later when I got home I went into the bathroom and dropped my drawers to view the damage in the mirror, and what I saw on my hinder was a hematoma the size of a personal pan pizza, framed by four angry red fang marks. First thing I thought was, *Man, I gotta show somebody!* So I hollered for my wife and told her to bring the camera. You get festooned up with an injury of this caliber, you want some documentation for the grandkids.

It hurt to sit and it hurt to walk, but I wanted to get those pigs turned out before the rabies hit, so I backed the pickup over to the paddock I'd set up and turned them loose. I took them out of the back of the pickup, and it was really neat to see them hit the dirt. They started snuffling and snorting and rolling around. My daughter Amy, seven at the time, was watching them and then all of a sudden she said, "Oh, Daddy, they're so cute! I'm calling that one Wilbur and that one Cocklebur!" I said, "Well, honey, that's okay, but you have to understand that in October we're going to turn the pigs into food." I wasn't sure if she really got it. But a few weeks later we had some cousins visit from the city. Amy took them down to see the pigs while I fetched the slop bucket, so I got there a little late. Just as I walked up she was pointing at the pigs. "That one over there is Wilbur and that one's Cocklebur," she said, "but in October that one's Ham and that one's Bacon."

These days most of the food in our freezer and the eggs in our skillet do come from our own little farm. But nope, I'm not really a farmer. I'm a self-employed storyteller with part-time pigs. And if I get home tomorrow and find out all they've all croaked, well, it's not the end of my career. It's just a bad weekend.

And one more story to tell.

HAUTE PIG FEED

I try to feed my pigs on the cheap. With the price of corn these days, that's a challenge. We do buy them a little hog feed, mainly because I like to hang out at the feed mill and pretend that I'm a farmer too. As if I owned five hundred pigs, not five. Right above the honor system candy box they've got a television monitor where the weather report always runs with the sound off. I like to stare at it mournfully, because that's what farmers do: they stare at the weather report mournfully. When the other farmers complain about the price of pork bellies, I nod in agreement, then as soon as I'm in the pickup I check my smartphone to figure out, what exactly are pork bellies again?

Mostly our pigs graze. People forget sometimes that pigs are grazers. They love to eat young nettles and fresh crabgrass. And most of all, of course, they love to root around. They're organic bulldozers. Mostly they go after roots, but I've also watched a two-hundred-pound pig tease out an angleworm using his almost prehensile lower lip. When the worm was balanced just right, he sucked it down like spaghetti.

But they won't be fat by October on worms and crabgrass alone, so we supplement wherever we can. They get our table scraps, of course. We collect them in a bucket. My poor daughters may be children of the digital age, but they are very familiar with the old analog phrase, "Slop the hogs."

We plant patches of field peas and rape, the plant used to make canola oil (it's like cabbage that doesn't roll up), and feed it to them by the wheelbarrowful. We also buy them expired baked goods at the local bakery outlet. Our neighbors who raise goats give us the leftover milk; we mix it in with the bakery castoffs and the pigs gobble it right down. We store the excess goat milk in plastic carboys. We don't refrigerate it, we just keep it right out by the pen. By the time you get to the bottom of the barrel, things are getting mighty cheesy. I get the gaggers, but it doesn't slow those pigs at all.

Unfortunately, the baked goods have lately become scarce. Back in the early days of my pig-raising career I could sometimes score an entire pickup truck bed full of hot dog, hamburger, and bratwurst buns, bagels, and the occasional crate of chocolate frosted mini-doughnuts, all for around twelve bucks. These days that's next to impossible. Part of the reason is that bear hunters buy up a lot of the sticky buns and doughnuts and such and use them for bait. Also, more and more people are raising their own pigs and chickens, so competition for the expired goods has increased. And finally, times are tough: although the expired goods are clearly labeled ANIMAL FEED ONLY, as a guy who has fished more than one mini-doughnut out of the pile I can tell you that expired or not, that food will still do a human just fine.

So we've had to expand our reach to scavenge free pig food. Last weekend I was able to swing a deal with a coffee shop that does a big high-end breakfast business on the weekends. Late Sunday afternoon, after the restaurant portion of the shop closed down, I pulled up with my pickup truck and the kitchen crew helped me carry out three bags of delicious food garbage. When I dumped the bags in the trough, what spilled out was a buffet: fresh diced vegetables, raisin bagels, rye bread, chunked fresh fruit, blueberry syrup, leftover three-cheese omelet, and—best of all—several lemon ricotta crepes.

Boy, those pigs dove right in, snout first, feet to follow. Every now and then they'd jostle around and trade places, wedging themselves into a new spot, perhaps hoping to get a scrap of blueberry buckwheat pancake or a scallion.

When it was over they retired to the pig hutch and flopped in a pile like a friendly cluster of overstuffed bratwurst. They looked so comfortable I felt I should offer each of them a double cappuccino. Happily, they are pigs, and pigs' tastes run on a sliding scale; as soon as the crepes wore off they went right back to eating worms.

SKUNK WAR

I got done with work real late the other night—sometime after midnight—and when I walked across the yard toward the house I noticed a light coming from the open granary door.

I decided to check it out, because we have chicks in the granary. They're kept beneath a protective screen, but a good strong coon or an industrious chicken-craving critter might still get at them. Plus, after feeding and watering them this afternoon the absent-minded writer who plays at being a farmer may have forgotten to weigh down the screen with the standard three bricks and two chunks of firewood.

So I detoured over there. As I approached the doorway I remember thinking, *Smells like skunk,* but it didn't really register until I stepped inside and there he was.

He was a beady-eyed little feller, blinking at me from behind the pitchforks. I'm told that skunks have very poor eyesight. (I'm not sure who's in charge of officially checking these things. Are there volunteer veterinary ophthalmologists who head out into the forest with miniature eye charts? I'm seeing the skunk reclined against a stump holding that little black plastic paddle over one eye while the ophthalmologist stands there in a white smock very patiently saying, "Okay, let's try that top row one more time." And the skunk is squinting real hard and thinking to himself, *Y'know, I've heard a lot of good things about this Lasik surgery . . .*)

The point is, I regarded that skunk with no ill will, but knowing full well he could not see well enough to discern my intent, I figured I'd just back off and let him work it out. Sure enough, he headed across the granary, but just as I thought he was going to exit the open door he hung a right and headed for the old horse stall where the chicks are kept.

Now, we keep the chicks in a stock tank under a heat lamp. And because of the weighted screen, that skunk isn't going to get to them. But the chicks were cheeping nervously, and I didn't want to close the doors and leave him in there to fumigate the place until morning. I also didn't want to leave the doors open all night, as there are raccoons about.

Here is the thing: how do you get a skunk out of a horse stall? Clearly the direct approach was no good. Whenever I eased toward him his tail went up, and ten seconds later I'd be beating feet out the door for a gulp of fresh air. I tried tossing pebbles and empty feed bags, but although this made him jump a few times, in the end he just hunkered down. At one point I left the granary and gave him five minutes to himself, but when I returned he had curled up next to the wall and was gazing steadily—if blindly—at the tank of chicks. Eyeing them with bad intent, as Jethro Tull would have it.

The impasse finally broke when I let myself into the adjacent stall and banged on the divider. The divider is constructed of solid boards, which allowed me to be right next to the skunk but shielded from his perfume shooter. Unsettled by the noise and seeing his opening, the skunk ambled out of his stall, across the granary floor, and out the door.

I checked the chicks one more time, battened the hatches, and headed for the house.

I guess my favorite part of that whole story is how when that skunk finally made a break for it, he just toddled along. I realize skunks can't sprint any more than they can read an eye chart, but it still was kinda neat to see that of the two of us, it was the big human that was the flummoxed one. And how you would have chuckled to see me peering around the corner of that stall, reeaaalll slow and tentative, and ready to go sprinting into the night.

Varmints are varmints—especially when they're eyeing your eggs and egg-makers—and I make no promises regarding future relations, but for that one night I was happy to see the skunk go, and go easy. I got off pretty light, scentwise—although I did stand in the midnight wind for a bit before crawling into bed with my wife—and no one has complained, but I do have visions of that skunk back at the little skunk tavern after a hard night of foraging and all of his skunk pals blinking blindly and wrinkling their noses, and then finally someone says, "Hey, who smells like scared human?"

E-I-IPO

Out back on the farm the other morning I was thinking this is quite a world we live in, because while I was feeding the pigs a particularly pungent trough of swill I was simultaneously listening to an international business news show on my telephone. One could draw certain parallels between the international business scene and a pig trough, but that is not my point and furthermore, let's play nice.

I wish I could tell you I listen to international business news shows because I'm making some really big moves in Malaysian Manganese futures or preparing for a treble-trillion-dollar IPO of my new social media site for lovers of exotic cheeses, but the truth is I like to listen to the international business news for the same reason I like to listen to John Coltrane or Lenny Bruce: I'm not sure exactly what I'm hearing, but it plays smoothly on the ear.

The thing is, I have only the most superficial understanding of what the hosts and guests are discussing. I hear them say things like "knock-on-effects going forward," "multiple equilibria," "earning beats," "the bar-belled approach," "short-end paper," and "snap-back," and I have no idea what it all means. But man, it has this great word-jazz groove. There I am slogging away with my five-gallon plastic buckets—the ones my buddy Mills rescued from the dump—with five pigs stomping on my toes and nibbling at my kneecaps, and in my ear some corporate captain or economic seer is purring confidently in the fluency of basis points, ten-year Treasuries, the fluctuations of NYMEX crude, the VIX, the S&P, and QE3.

Esoteric language—especially when used as offhand shorthand—always has its poetry, even if your understanding is pidgin. One of my favorite things is when my eighty-two-year-old neighbor Tom gets going on how he makes things on his lathe. He starts talking about babbits and collets and boring bars, and I don't quite follow, but the rhythm is mesmerizing. (Obviously I am not allowed near the lathe when it is actually turning.)

It isn't just the jazz of the business news I love, it's the sideways insight into what's happening in the world. All that economic esoterica speaks to subterranean backroom churnings and machinations and invisible rivers of power and money humming along, but even more importantly this talk can give you a sense of where the world is heading no matter what the politicians say. For all the shark-feeding and voodoo of the big whale investing world, on a daily basis—for better or worse—your bloodless stock analyst power broker will speak truths few folks seeking election will utter. You may learn why pig futures stand as they do, even though it won't change what you do with your own homegrown bacon. And yet, as the hosts and guests trade their jargon-y riffs, I feel like I'm being given a penny-stock peek through the smoked-glass window obscuring how the world really turns.

My favorite time to listen to this business talk is on deep winter mornings when our farm feels comfy, insulated, and isolated. After the chickens are fed and the coffee is fresh and I am early at the desk, I tune my phone to the live stream while I check the calendar and my email and maybe peck away at an essay or sort the bills.

The last time I listened a correspondent reported that Greece was wider by 32 basis points. That might be good, but probably not, because the follow-up interview included the terms *currency debasement, forced restructuring,* and—this'll really make you grab your pants—*adverse exogenous shock.*

I had one of those last year while checking the electric pig fence.

Sitting there in my little room over the garage, I envision the interviewees solidly desked in dark-paneled offices, comfortably corner-windowed in a gleaming tower, or discoursing over a cell-phone from the back of a Lincoln Town Car, and I contrast their life to mine. Sometimes I do wish I was being driven to work in a limousine, but looking across the yard I find I am fairly satis-fied with the arbitrage of fresh eggs and firewood. Your average international businessman might see nothin' but chickens and a chainsaw, but I see *means of re-capitalization.*

COCK-A-DOODLE-EGO

I had a little run-in with our rooster again.

We've just got the one rooster. It's him and about fifty-nine hens, so I figure he's either plumb happy or plumb tuckered or both. Actually I'm pretty sure he's not happy, because roosters just don't ever seem very happy. They're so busy strutting and fluffing and crowing and stomping around and generally doing everything they can to let you know they're the big boss man (while simultaneously trying to subjugate every hen within three square miles) that they never really seem to let their feathers down and just hang out.

The thing about a rooster is, if you're a man, sometimes when you're out there throwing cracked corn and you see the way that ridiculous bird sticks his feathered chest out and tries to stand taller than he is—especially when he just rares back and crows at nothing—this uncomfortable self-recognition thing happens. I mean, I've hit that stage in life where I've settled into a rela- tively mellow groove, and I'm certainly not looking for a fight, and yet sometimes I watch that rooster and recognize I am not completely cured of the strut and cock-a-doodle-doo.

When I was a kid we had a big white rooster. He used to home in on my sister like a heat-seeking beak missile, and she was for- ever screeching through the yard at sixty miles an hour with that rooster flapping and pecking all around her. Sometimes when we thought she needed a rest, my brother John and I would tackle him, and then we'd hypnotize him. The most artistic means of accomplishing this was to put him on the ground with his neck stretched, then draw a line repeatedly from his comb down his beak and about six inches straight out in the dirt. We'd do that a dozen times, then back slowly away, and that rooster would sit there, beached on his breast and blinking like he just crawled out of a mile-long mine shaft. Generally if you didn't disturb him he'd be out of commission for a good five or ten minutes. Then pretty soon you'd hear a howl and a cackle and that bird and my sister would be doing the Daytona 500 around the chicken coop again.

Sometimes for variety I'd peel the rooster off my sister's left calf and haul him up the ladder clear to the top of the feed bin, where I'd stand on the bin cap, tuck his head beneath one wing, rotate him in a circle, and pitch him into the air like a football. He'd usually be about ten feet off the ground before his head popped out and he got to windmilling. He was never injured—although he may have scuffed his beak—and furthermore this did nothing to deter him from attacking my sister, but for purposes of safety and so that I don't get angry letters, I cannot in good conscience recommend this to the subsequent generations.

All in all I am not a fan of male chickens. That said, I do like to hear a rooster crow in the morning. Twice. Then I wish he'd give it a rest. If you've ever had roosters, you know they crow at sunrise, they crow at moonrise, they crow at each other, they crow at their reflection in the coop window, they crow as soon as you turn your back to leave the chicken run, they just crow, crow, crow. Sometimes I crow back. And I stomp toward the rooster and keep crowing until he runs behind the coop. And then I look at the hens and stick my chest out a little bit and bounce my shoulders like I'm fluffing my feathers, and sure enough right about then that rooster sticks his head around the corner of the coop and crows again, and as I whirl to march back at him, I suddenly realize it is not the rooster who has the problem here.

SNOW PLOW TROUBLE

I recently had to recalibrate my attitude regarding snowstorms. I am compelled to admit that over time I have taken to making sport of those who get all ginned up over what we in Wisconsin should consider normal (and, in light of recent droughts, welcome) weather. Let there be the slightest whiff of snowflake, and the red alerts start popping up on your cellphone and crawling across your television screen while apparently terror-stricken reporters deliver headlines the likes of "Snow-Based Snowstorm Likely to Include Snow, So Watch Out for Snow" and "How to Choose Your Mittens." For the love of rock salt, I say, chuckling with disdain, it's just a little snow.

Then came a snowstorm I shall call the Great White Humbler.

It arrived early on a Sunday and stayed all day. The Green Bay Packers were playing a night game, and I wanted to clear the driveway at least once before settling in on the couch. Well, before I watched a single down of that football game, I was sacked by the snow, I was pinned deep in my own territory by the snow, I was taunted in the end zone by the snow, and, after establishing an insurmountable lead, the snow continued to run up the score.

Let's check the stats:

3:52 p.m.: Time I jumped in the plow truck and ran down the hill to help someone get up our hill in a mini-van.

1: Number of times I slid into the ditch with my four-wheel-drive plow truck while "helping" someone in a mini-van.

15: Factor by which I was stuck worse after "gunning it" to get out of the previous predicament. ("Gunning it" is known in some circles as "Rammin' on it.")

.2: Number of inches by which my plow blade missed hooking the telephone company's junction box when everything came to rest. (Time was called in order to count blessings, yea, even in this moment.)

1: Number of caps borrowed from mini-van driver in order to make long walk back up hill to fetch the tractor in driving snow because I was "just gonna run down there and back" and had thus dressed myself in the manner of a distracted seventh grader, meaning no jacket, no cap, and just one glove—which somehow seemed worse than no gloves at all.

500: BTUs of necessary warmth generated during hike back up hill during which the coals of self-loathing were fanned by gusts of futile rage.

17: Degrees required to measure the new angle of the bumper after the neighbor and I got done yanking the truck back on to the road.

5: Minutes passed before I had the truck stuck again, this time down by the barnyard.

16: Inches required to measure the length of the crease put in the quarter panel by the railroad tie fence post down by the barnyard, which apparently isn't going anywhere.

3: Total number of times I had to go ask my wife to put all her stuff on again and come help pull me out.

1: Total number of times right at the end there where I got the plow truck stuck after she had suggested I just park it and wait for daylight.

0: Exact number of times I asked her for help that time and

instead just put the truck in neutral and yanked it out with the tractor all by myself.

1: Number of knots jerked into the brand new tow rope during that last little adventure.

7:52 p.m.: Exact time I just gave up and went in to watch the Packers game.

The Eskimos have a word for snow like this. It is not printable.

REALLY FREE-RANGE CHICKEN

Back home on the farm I've been dealing with that one chicken. You know, that one chicken, the one that's never where she's supposed to be.

We free-range our chickens in the early spring, but once asparagus and gardening season kick in we switch over to a portable chicken fence. Nothing is more disheartening than spending the newborn morning nestling tender seedlings into the welcoming earth only to wander out over a reflective afternoon lemonade to find the whole works scratched into oblivion by a gang of marauding cluckers. When we first started raising chickens, many people happily told me the birds would keep pests out of the garden. What they didn't tell me is they would also strip the rutabagas, strafe the string beans, claw up the garlic, and peck the eyes out of the potatoes. To be fair, they do take a break now and then to poop on the deck. I'll tell you how to keep pests out of the garden: LOCK UP THE CHICKENS.

So now we have a fairly workable deal combining a coop on wheels and the aforementioned portable fence. I let the birds out on fresh ground in the morning, they get to peck and scratch and hunt bugs just the way they're designed, and we get to keep our kale. Meanwhile, I go up to work in my little office over the garage. But this year a pattern has emerged. By 10 a.m. or so I spy a barred rock hen come easing out around from behind the granary, free-range as you please.

The first time I figured it was a fluke. I caught her and put her back in. I made that sound easy, but it wasn't. Before it was over both the chicken and I were out of breath and making angry squawking noises. Sometimes farmers need track shoes. I went back to work. And an hour later there she was again. I checked the entire fence perimeter for holes or gaps. Nothing. Plus, those other forty-nine chickens—including identical breeds with identical wingspans and theoretically identical brainpans—were staying put.

It's been a week now, and I still haven't figured it out. That chicken and I have gone sixteen rounds. She's lost some feathers and I've lost some patience. The thing that really drives me nuts is that I can't actually catch her in the act. She's either in or she's out. Because of where we're grazing them, the coop isn't visible from where I'm working, and naturally if I hang around spying on her, she stays put. I have entertained the idea of rigging a webcam so I can monitor her remotely, but we have real bad internet, plus these are the moments when you realize you're starting to go a little Captain Ahab over the whole deal.

I have come to the conclusion that what we've got here is a shape-shifting chicken. Yesterday, right on schedule, she tippy-toed out from behind the granary and slipped down between the spruce trees to peck around in the brush below the pole barn. I've seen a fox down there lately, so that chicken may be about to solve this problem herself. Passing through a fox is pretty much the ultimate shape-shift.

In the meantime, I bolt from the desk now and then to see if I can catch her in transit, but she's always either in or out. So far she hasn't attacked the garden. Perhaps that's a team sport, and she doesn't want to proceed without the other chickens. And therein lies the final indignity: every time I stand there all befuddle-faced, studying the fence, trying to work out how that dang Houdini-bird does it, there are forty-nine sets of beady eyes staring right back at me, and every single one of them knows the answer. You know what makes an evil sound? Forty-nine snickering chickens.

PATHFINDING

*During the musical portion of this show, a group of singer-
songwriters sat on the stage going around the circle playing
songs, some of which dated back to the days of the troubadors.*

I was walking from my writing room over the garage toward the
house the other day when I noticed I've begun wearing a path in
the grass between the two buildings.

That shallow little rut makes me happy. I don't know how long
we'll live on this farm, but it's good to know I've been here long
enough to scuff some paths into the dirt.

I know all about the negative connotations of the rut—
metaphorical and otherwise—but in a world where the perfectly
tended lawn seems to represent the pinnacle of civility, I prefer a
well-worn path here and there. Back when I was a kid haying on
the Jerry Coubal farm, I used to love walking the dirt path that
ran from Jerry's farmhouse to his barn. It cut a good three inches
into the sod and ran arrow-straight. Jerry's people were Eastern
European immigrants who came here with nothing. By the time I
was old enough to help hoist his hay bales, Jerry had one of the
finest farms in the county. I figure one of the reasons for that was
because of that straight path. When Jerry left the house for the
barn he quite literally went straight to work.

We had paths on our farm too. My favorites were the ones
worn by the cows and sheep across the pastures. Perhaps these
paths didn't reflect best grazing practices, but they did reflect a

natural rhythm in which the animals came and went with the sun, and the way the paths forked and forked again and eventually faded into the grass was the same as the veining of green leaves, an organic pattern reassuring to the eye.

Not all paths are worn in the dirt. Back in the day my neighbor Tom used to run a matched pair of oxen. His best pair were named Chester and Lester. They pulled in more than twenty-five parades, Tom says. He started making yokes for Chester and Lester when they were calves. He says he learned how to do it by reading Foxfire books. By the time Chester and Lester were full grown they went about twenty-four-hundred pounds apiece; the yoke alone was six feet wide and weighed nearly sixty pounds. Tom hand-carved the beam and made the bows from red elm he cut from the river bottoms. He'd steam them over a hog kettle of boiling water and bend them using a homemade jig. Things didn't always work perfectly.

Over in the corner of Tom's workshop there is a spade with a handle shaped like an upside-down "U." If you jab the spade blade into the dirt, the handle rises up, then curves around and drops so that the butt of the handle is pointing straight back down at the earth. One of Tom's favorite things is to take a newcomer through his workshop, and just before the newcomer is ready to leave, Tom will grab that shovel and hold it up. "Whaddaya think this is?" he'll ask. And after the guest hazards a guess or two, Tom's eyes will twinkle, he'll grin, and he'll say, "I picked this shovel up from the ditch after the boys on the country road crew got done leanin' on it!" And then he'll cackle like it's the freshest joke he's heard in a year.

Tom performed the shovel joke for me for the first time right around the time we moved to the farm. I bet I've seen him do it for other unsuspecting newbies fifteen times since. And I know full well that the U-shaped shovel handle is actually one of Tom's failed oxbows. But I never get tired of watching him set the whole joke up and then deliver it with that sly twinkle he gets. That story is a well-worn path, and it's a good one.

Perhaps the most precious gift of a well-worn path is how it reminds us we have been blessed with a stretch of no disruption. Some measure of peaceful continuity. That is why it is good to hear these singers this evening. The songs they're sharing in the tent tonight are not being sung for the first time. In some cases they've been sung multitudes of times over tens of thousands of miles and decades or even centuries. But every time they emanate from the stage it is like the first time. There are some things—good saddle leather, a shovel handle, a soothing chorus, those old footpaths—that don't get worn out, they get worn in.

FRIENDS AND NEIGHBORS

Friends and neighbors. It's good when they're both.

THE CUTTING EDGE

I was talking with my neighbor Tom the other day. I admit I was bragging a little, telling him about my new scythe. I think you pronounce the *th,* but I'm not sure. For years I went around pronouncing it "sigh," hoping that was somehow more high-tone, but Tom says scythe with a full-blown *th* so lately I've been going with that.

Tom is eighty-two years old now. Lives in the same house he was born in. Just never came up with any real good reason to leave, I guess. He's got a nice little farm there down by the crick. Well, it used to be down by the crick, but then one day in 1967 Dwight D. Eisenhower's interstate came plowing through about a hay bale toss from the barn and now there's a three-mile detour between the porch and the crick, but that's a story for another book.

I met Tom while I was dating my ultimate girlfriend. I call her the ultimate girlfriend because she was, but also because ultimately I married her. Or she married me. (I should check the paperwork.)

My ultimate girlfriend used to bale hay for Tom. One day fairly early in the courtship Tom pulled me aside and told me she outworked every boy he ever hired. He seemed to intend this less as a testament to her character than a challenge to my own.

Tom has seen it all from oxcarts up to the internet, which he just recently began to surf. I spend a little time with him now and then when I need something welded or turned on the metal lathe, or if I'm just looking for advice on how to comport myself over the long term.

So we're walking through his machine shed recently and I see a scythe slung up in the rafters. I start rhapsodizing about my own scythe, which I admit I am inordinately proud of, in part because it was won at an auction by my buddy Mills. (The formative years of our friendship were based on shooting carp with bows and arrows, but lately we've bonded over an addiction for auctions.)

So I'd told Mills I needed a scythe, and one day when he was going to one auction and I was going to another I got a call from him.

"You still lookin' for a scythe?"

"Thaaat's affirmative." (Two decades, and we still like to pretend we're talking on our fire radios.)

"What'll y'go fer one? There's a beauty here, and they're starting the bidding!"

This was tough because pickers and rural theme restaurants have driven up the price. So I'm kinda mulling it over and Mills hollers in my ear. "I GOT IT!!!"

That was fast. Too fast. "Umm . . . whad'ya pay for it?"

"FIVE DOLLARS!" You should know that Mills regularly speaks in ALL CAPS.

"Five dollars? What kinda shape is it—"

"SHE'S A BEAUT!"

"Are you sur—"

"MINT!"

Part of the fun of this story is imagining the scene on the other end of the phone: Mills with his eyes the size of canning lids, surrounded by the auction crowd and hollering into his cellphone and dancing over a five-dollar scythe. It's like the redneck version of Sotheby's, when they have those unidentified bidders calling in from Monaco or Macau, or Chippewa County or whatever.

So I wind up with this scythe, and it is a beauty. I use it mostly for cutting wheat and oats, which I then harvest by hand and put up in the granary for the chickens over winter. I've even learned how to sharpen it. I have three different whetstones, and I use them in sequence. The fine grit stone was quarried in Slovakia, and I think that's probably important. I like sharpening the blade while the sweat runs down my brow. Makes me feel hardy.

Now I'm in the machine shed with Tom, and I see his scythe up there in the rafters and I start rattling on about my scythe. I tell him how I sharpen it. I tell him how I use it to cut the oats and wheat to feed the chickens, and I describe my sharpening technique and ask him what he thinks of it. All this time he's just looking at me with a quiet smile, and I know what that quiet smile says: it says how pleased he is that some of us in the trailing generations are taking up the old ways, respecting them and nurturing them and carrying them forward. When he looks up in the rafters at that trusty old scythe of his and says, "Yep, sounds like you're doin' it about right," my heart swells with pride.

Then he lowers his gaze back to meet mine, and he smiles, and he says, "Y'know what else works real good?"

I'm all ears, ready for the wisdom.

"Yah, one'a them gas-powered weed-whackers!"

Everything old is new again. Then we remember why it was we ditched the old things in the first place . . .

FRIENDLY FENCING

I took my two daughters on a hike the other day.

The highlight of the trip came when we sat down on a stump for snack time and spotted a big ol' bear track in the mud. You could see it all: the individual pads, the tippy-tip claw marks, and most entertaining of all, a greasy sideways smear leading up to it, so you know he lost his footing and slipped coming in. There was much giggling during my reenactment of what a big tough bear looks like when it slips in the mud, including how he ducks his head and looks around to see if anyone was watching.

During the hike we discovered that a big old willow tree at the end of the valley had blown down across the neighbor's fence and was blocking his gate. So the next day I called my buddy Mills and we cut it up. I called Mills because it's good to have help for a project like that, but also because my wife and daughters were gone that day, and we have a rule about never going out into the woods with a chainsaw unless someone is around to hear you if you need help. I made that rule because I come from a family of loggers and know what can go wrong—especially if you're more familiar with a keyboard than a chainsaw. Mills has that rule because the last time he ran his chainsaw without someone around he got pinched in a tree and had a long wait before taking an ambulance ride.

Before we went out I sharpened my chain. I placed the saw on the luggage rack of the four-wheeler, which is just the right height for running the file through the teeth. The four-wheeler was parked down by the pole barn, and I had the door open and the shop radio tuned to a station that plays songs ranging from Sinatra to Jimmy Buffet to Peabo Bryson. When Mills pulled in the yard I told him I couldn't imagine a better life, just standing there in the good weather sharpening a saw chain on the luggage rack of a four-wheeler while easy music floats out the pole barn door.

When the saws were gassed and oiled, we loaded up our gear and headed down-valley.

My neighbor down that way has been farming for longer than I've been living. The old rules say, when you're standing facing a line fence, the right-hand half is your responsibility. These days things tend to get more legalistic, but when I've got an old-school neighbor I'm happy to operate in the old-school manner. Last year I spent a full day trimming back our half of the fence. There was one tree too big to handle on my own, so the neighbor in question drove over with his big farm tractor and we did the job together. It was the first time we'd ever really met. After the tree was cut up and dragged clear and the brush was stacked, we had a nice five-minute visit, and what you had there was your basic rural Welcome Wagon moment.

The neighbor hadn't called about the downed willow yet, and that's part of the reason I got down here as soon as I could with Mills. There's something to be said for filling a request before it's made. It's a way to let him know I'm paying attention and trying to be a good neighbor. I don't know if I'm being altruistic or prideful in that respect, but anyways, here we are.

It didn't take us long to limb and block the thing up, although by the time we got everything dragged and stacked we were both sweating heavily. Then we took our saws and ran the rest of the fenceline, trimming things here and there, pulling a few limbs off the barbwire.

Before we packed up our gear, we took a moment to just stand there and look at the empty space where the willow tree had been. The post-project lookover is a classic male ceremony. No job is really finished until you bask in it a little. You'll see the same thing with a guy who has just finished shoveling the driveway or stacking firewood. Backed up three steps, hands on hips, gazing upon What He Hath Wrought.

And then we went on to the rest of the day. I slept well that night, in part from all the chainsawing and wood-lugging. But the rest also came easy because I know the next time my neighbor and I meet on the road, I can nod at him and he can nod at me because of the fact—rather than in spite of the fact—that a good fence stands between us.

TRUCK TALK

Lately the price of feeder pigs is way up. I did not get this information from the market report, I did not check it on the web, I got the news the way a guy oughta get that kind of news: through two pickup truck windows.

I got my first pigs from my neighbor Mike: two of them for forty dollars apiece, and feeders run roughly forty pounds. So, about a buck a pound. Last week I was running to the feed mill, and when I went past Mike's place he was about to leave the yard in his pickup truck so I figured I'd check to see if he had any feeders for sale this year. I pulled into his driveway, and we lined up our doors and lowered our windows and we convened a meeting. I think it'd be neat if you could track all the business conducted through pickup truck windows over the years. 'Course, if you wanted to get the true average you'd probably have to figure in all the time *wasted* through pickup truck windows over the years, but let's not get statistical.

Mike's driveway worked fine, but your classic pickup window chat takes place over a center line. I love the ceremonial process of it: how you recognize the oncoming vehicle and you slow down and then you just ease up to each other until those windows align. Then you kill the engines and shoot the breeze while the flies buzz. You talk about where you're headed, you talk about where you're coming from, you talk about how the corn is looking, and you keep one eye out for traffic. If a car approaches and you're at a point in the story where you can wrap it up, you crank the starter, roll off, and toss a "See y'later!" out the window. But if you're in the middle of the good part of a story, you know, like what the guy at the feed mill said about the milk inspector's ex-wife's new boyfriend, the one with the glass eye and the International Harvester tattoo (I mean here to refer to the boyfriend, not the ex-wife or the milk inspector), what you do then is you pull ahead just enough to let them weave their way through and then you back up, realign, and pick up where you left off.

Usually you just chitchat and talk smart, what you call a "smoke & joke." But sometimes you get real nuggets. It was through pickup truck windows at the intersection of Carlson Corners that I received the happy news of my brother Jed's engagement.

Unfortunately not everybody gets it anymore, and I have a perpetually renewing resolution not to hold daily funerals for the past so I'm not going to saw on this for too long, but I knew things had changed a while back when I was still living in my hometown of New Auburn. There were only 485 people in residence and Main Street is wide enough you could run five wide NASCAR-style with room left over for Willie Johnson to ride his lawn mower to the tavern. I was out cutting grass one day and my buddy Snake drove by. He stopped, so I walked out there in the middle of Main Street and leaned into his window. We talked for a pretty good stretch. Every now and then someone would drive through and they'd just swing around us, no big deal. Then this woman pulls right up on Snake's bumper and she lays on the horn. I looked at her and then slowly rolled my eyes around the space surrounding us as if to say, *You know, Ma'am, you just have at 'er. Roll right around us.* Then I went back to visiting with Snake. The woman honked again. Snake and I just kept visiting.

Finally the woman gave the steering wheel a violent twist, stomped the accelerator, and whipped out around us. As she zoomed past, she flew us the bird.

We gave her the gaze.

Our point being, Ma'am, this is how we hold neighborly visits around here in lieu of a garden fence. And when you stop to visit through a pickup truck window, you are luxuriating in the tapering moments of a quieter time. And furthermore, honking crabs the soul.

So Mike and I, we had a nice visit in his driveway. Unfortunately, he doesn't have any feeder pigs for me this year. As a matter of fact, he's looking for some himself and he tells me that the cheapest ones he's found are sixty dollars apiece, which is a bit of a shock after they've held steady at forty for so many years now.

That was bad news. But if you're gonna get bad farmin' news, you might as well get it from a neighbor who's in the same boat. Or in the same pickup truck, as it were. And talking to you through a rolled-down window.

We drove off and went about our business. I stopped by the feed mill and bought chicken feed. While the feed mill man was tallying up the bill, I leaned against the feed mill counter and we commiserated about the price of pigs. In the absence of a pickup truck window, the feed mill counter is a fine substitute.

JOHN DEERE FUNERAL

It's been a year since Donnie died. He was a neighbor I didn't know real well or for a real long time, but knew well enough to know his name and know his truck and wave when I saw him plowing his sweet corn patch with his beloved Johnny-Popper.

A couple years back the township trimmed the trees along our road, and Donnie and his brother Denny (Denny lives right down the hill from me) got the crew to drag the trees to a spot out there behind Denny's shop. They'd peck away at the pile now and then, but with fall coming on and quite a few sticks to go, they said if I'd come down there and give them a hand I could take some of that firewood. Donnie was already in the fight of his life by then—cancer—but when I showed up with my pickup and trailer there he was, leaning on the back of the buzz saw, ready to go.

The buzz saw was homemade and painted John Deere green and yellow, because those brothers are John Deere through and through. Always have been. I'm more an International Harvester guy, but when there is wood to be made you join the team, and besides, with that blade spinning right there a guy isn't going to quibble over colors.

We worked steadily but carefully; when you grow up where and when I did the very term *buzz saw* brings to mind old-timers short three fingers, and those were the happy accidents. The wood bolts were stacked fairly neatly, but there was still a quite a little tugging and lugging to be done, as if we were undoing a pile of giant jackstraws. I lugged the long chunks, Denny tossed the sawn chunks, and Donnie worked the saw bed back and forth. We kept an eye on him but he looked good the whole time, and when it was done I had two heaping loads, the truck and trailer springs sagging.

I didn't see Donnie a lot after that—waved at him a time or two and inquired as to his condition whenever I talked to Denny—but I knew he was struggling, up and down. When I saw the obituary I couldn't say I was surprised.

The funeral was held in a small town nearby, and I wasn't sure exactly which church was hosting the service, but the town was of a size that all I had to do was peek down two or three streets until I saw where all the cars were, and that was the place. When the church part was over they bore his casket to the cemetery on a hay wagon drawn by one of his antique John Deere tractors. You could hear it coming from clear the other side of the railway tracks, the pop-pop-pop, slow and steady.

It turned cold the day of the funeral, cold enough that despite the green grass, when I got back home I stoked a fire in the woodstove. When we were buzz-sawing wood that day, we cut some of those chunks a little long before we got 'er dialed in, and so as I was trying to wedge a section of split maple into the firebox on the diagonal—the only way it would fit—I recognized it as a piece Donnie helped us cut that day, one of the many that kept us warm all winter long, and as the kindling took and the smoke curled up and out into the chill air I figured there are a lot of ways to honor a man.

AMBULANCE KARMA

I left the farm the other night and drove into town to the local technical college to begin my biannual first responder refresher. Every two years we have to revisit and retest on all the ways there are to keep people ticking when they've stopped tocking. The refresher is twenty-eight hours of classroom time and usually takes place over a month or so, and I always run into trouble stringing one together because I'm on the road a bunch, not that that makes me special, because there are truckers and soldiers in the department who face the very same scheduling issues. I realize I just said being a soldier causes "scheduling issues" and will think on that some more later. Jeepers.

Anyways, as we say around here when we aren't saying Any-*hoo,* the local emergency services instructors have kindly helped me work out a schedule that fits in between all the road days, and I'm spending a lot of time looking at PowerPoints about how to administer epinephrine and oral glucose and practicing splinting pretend broken arms and treating fake shock and binding up imaginary hemorrhages, and—because this is the modern age—rehearsing what to do in the event someone drops a weapon of mass destruction in the back yard.

You might think all this difficult-to-schedule death and destruction playacting would be a breathless downer, but actually, once I get in the classroom I really enjoy it. I'm closing in on my own quarter-century of being a volunteer EMT, first responder, and firefighter, and it's been a consistent part of my life longer than anything else in my life besides breathing. It's a privilege to serve alongside my neighbors wherever I may be. I love that we converge on scene with all of our different backgrounds and beliefs and abilities and suddenly start speaking in the same language: the language of rescue. The language of help.

I also cherish how the fire and rescue world exists in its own little space outside the things I do to make a living. All the writing and performing and running hither and yon, and yet when I step in that classroom and see the legless, armless BigHead mannequin lying there on the table with his hair that looks like bad chocolate frosting and his teeth that click if you put too much pressure on them while inserting an airway, well, then I know that it's time to practice inserting airways, in particular a CombiTube, and I know that if I meet another emergency medical provider somewhere even far from home and we don't know a thing about each other, if I say, "Inflate the blue tube first," he or she will smile and say, "And don't forget to auscultate for bilateral lung sounds and gastric insufflation," and we'll know exactly what we're talking about just as reliably as two poets talking villanelles or musicians talking minor fifths.

It just seems healthy to pursue some interest outside your main interests. In my case, being a volunteer rescue member has always been my way of reminding myself that I am mortal and ought to act that way. That trouble can come to any of us, in sixty-'leven different ways and at any time. Again, it sounds like a downer, but it doesn't feel like a downer. It feels solid to know that. Like the big surprise is pre-sprung, so it won't hit quite so hard when it comes. Or at least I'll recognize it for what it is and say, "Oh, it's the big surprise. Okay, then."

There's karma involved, too. Not the kind of karma where I believe if I make enough emergency calls I'll build up some cosmic bank account of get-out-of-jail-free cards, but rather the karma that when the day comes when I need help—or, even more importantly and specific to my heart and situation, my family needs help, and it's one of those many days when I'm far from home—well, then, when help arrives it'll have a friendly face.

If you don't know what a CombiTube is, it doesn't matter. It's enough to know that it's a tube we use to help air go in and out when air isn't going in and out. That's all we really want, isn't it? To keep the air going in and out? And to know that if we're having trouble making the air go in and out—literally, sure, but even more frequently figuratively—someone will come around to lend a hand.

TOM AND ARLENE IN LOVE

I was over visiting my neighbors Tom and Arlene a while back and we were talking about how life tends to roll around in circles . . . although not perfect circles. Maybe it'd be more accurate to say life is elliptical. With an ellipse you get a little more wiggle room, and goodness knows the secret to happiness is a little more wiggle room.

I love to visit Tom and Arlene. Tom is eighty-two and spry; Arlene is a few years younger but her health is not the best. Often when we talk she is using oxygen, and you can hear the hiss of the tank in the background. Tom and Arlene have been married fifty-nine years now. Arlene says her goal has always been to make it to their sixtieth anniversary. Even with the strain of recent hospital stays showing on her face, you can see the resolve in her eyes.

Sixty years of marriage. It's nowhere near a world record, but it deserves a tip of the seed corn cap, that's for sure. I tried pinning Tom down once on love and how to find it and how to make it last, but for all his knowledge—Tom is one of the smartest fellows I've ever known—he turns into a silly seventh grader when you try to get serious with him on matters of life and love.

"Why do you figure you and Arlene were able to make it last so long, Tom?" I ask him.

"Weahhll, I always say love is a disease everyone gets," he says. Then after waiting for a beat, he said, "Some people catch it quite often!"

Then he leaned forward in his chair and giggled at his own joke like a kid who just said something mildly naughty to his teacher, and it occurred to me that that attitude right there maybe had a lot to do with why he was still riding his bicycle a half a mile out to the mailbox and back every day at the age of eighty-two. The other day he told me, "I always tell people, I get up in the morning with nothin' to do, and by nighttime I'm only half done."

I had a point to make about those circles, but I got off track and am running out of time. One of my favorite things about visiting Tom and Arlene is how time slides into irrelevance. Well, not complete irrelevance, because they have a cuckoo clock on the wall and it doesn't really go tick-tock-tick-tock, it goes squeak-tock-squeak-tock and then of course every once in a while the little door slams open and that bird shoots out to give a crazed toot or two, but rather than making you feel like you should be getting back to business in the real world, the clockworks yank the bird back out of sight and the message seems to be: Never mind, I can come back again later, go ahead and visit, life is a circle. Or an ellipse. Or a zigzag. Take your pick, and take your time.

IN THE WAKE OF THE WAKE

Arlene did live to see her sixtieth wedding anniversary. She was fully present, and she celebrated in joy. A few months later she died at home, as she had also wished. To her last breath, Tom was at her side.

I went over to see my neighbor Tom the other evening. He recently lost his wife of some sixty years. I don't know how you quantify such a thing. I don't know how you remark on the echoes of such a departure without coming up short or obvious. I don't know that you even try.

I brought Tom a leftover pork chop that my wife had cooked. She and I are coming up on nine years married. I was thirty-nine when we took our vows, so barring my somehow making it to the century mark I'll likely not see sixty years of wedded union even if she'll have me that long. Tom thanked me for the pork chop and put it in the fridge with the other food accumulated since the funeral. It's only been a matter of weeks since Arlene died, so folks still drop in with a little something now and then, but Tom says it's tapering some, and I'm reminded of the friend who once told me, "The tough times start when the last casserole dish is returned." We were speaking in the wake of the funeral for my brother's first wife. He lost her just seven weeks into their marriage.

With the pork chop in reserve, Tom and I sat on wooden chairs in the kitchen. The room smelled faintly of bacon, and

I could see the pan over there on the stove. Tom said he had taken advantage of two warm days to get some of the garden in, although he thought it was probably too early, as it was turning cold again, but he just felt like he had to get out there and put something in the dirt. Bought his seed up at Stockman Farm Supply, he said, and he's going to try growing some of those dipper gourds this year. That and some new radish he's never seen in all his eighty-plus years. He's had a black bear coming around again, and he wonders if it's the one he ran out of the yard last fall. There he was, an octogenarian clad in nothing but a pair of cut-offs, swinging a stick and hollering at that bear to get out of the birdseed while Arlene rolled her eyes in the kitchen. He hasn't actually seen the bear this spring, but one of his bird feeders was sprung and one of his beehives was busted.

Last year Tom lent me a book about gunpowder, and along with the pork chop I had finally brought the book back. As it sat on the kitchen table between us we marveled at the miracle of saltpeter and sulfur and charcoal combined and then meandered off on a joint stem-winder examining humans and history and the unwavering dedication mankind has maintained in refining the means of killing one another. The discussion wound up with that moment where you both just sit there and shake your head, a morose sort of unity that is unity nonetheless.

We shot the breeze a good forty-five minutes before I asked Tom how his spirits were. That was when he told me about the bacon he made that morning. He said it was the first batch he'd fried up since Arlene died, and the minute it hit the pan the scent and sizzle hit him pretty hard, as he always fried one slice for him and one for her.

Later I thought about my brother losing his wife after seven weeks and Tom after sixty years and how these griefs might compare. It's an unanswerable question, I suppose, and not mine to speculate. The immediately bereaved are the only ones qualified to have that conversation. I have said that both men "lost" their wives, when in fact from what I have seen in their eyes it is they the living who are left lost.

As for the rest of us, we feel our way, trying to help, not really knowing how but hoping that maybe by sitting in the kitchen chair and conversing about nothing much and sharing in the sense of absence without necessarily saying so, we might somehow shine some dim light on the path forward.

ACKNOWLEDGMENTS

Thanks to

Terry, Tom, Becky, and the entire Lake Superior Big Top
Chautauqua bunch, from the Blue Canvas Orchestra
and singers to stage and sound crew and all
board members and volunteers

Jaime Hansen, who brings the studio
right on out to the farm

Alissa Freeberg, for remarkable and
conscientious assistance

Blakeley Beatty, for booking it

Karen Rose, for those other books

Kate, Kathy, Kristin, Elizabeth, and Ted at the
Wisconsin Historical Society Press

John and Beth at the *Wisconsin State Journal*

Al Ross, microphone sensei

Lisa and Dan at ICM

And my family, the ones I think of every time I say,
"Back home on the farm . . ."

ABOUT THE AUTHOR

....

Michael Perry is the author of numerous books, including *Population: 485, Truck: A Love Story*, and the *New York Times* bestseller *Visiting Tom*. His live humor recordings include *Never Stand Behind a Sneezing Cow* and *The Clodhopper Monologues*. He lives in rural Wisconsin with his wife and daughters and is privileged to serve as a first responder with the local fire department. He can be found online at www.sneezingcow.com.